Embracing

Embracing Bliss

108 Daily Meditations

Jeff Kober

Red Crow Press 2022

979-8-9856010-0-8 ebook
979-8-9856010-2-2 paperback

To connect with Jeff and receive daily meditations in your inbox, please visit:
www.jeff-kober.com

Quotes from "I Am That: Talks with Sri Nisargadatta Maharaj" used by
permission from The Acorn Press

Quotes from "The Truth Is" by Sri H. W. L. Poonja used by permission from
Red Wheel/Weiser

Cover design by www.onegraphica.com
Cover photo by Jeff Kober

For all the readers through all the years
who said these words mattered,
and for Sri M

Praise for Embracing Bliss

I've been unbelievably fortunate to have sustained an increasingly prosperous career as an entertainer for more than twenty years now, but increased success has not increased my happiness. In fact, I found myself so gripped by anxiety and stress, that I became desperate for relief which I now find in meditation. Jeff Kober is my teacher, and the contents of this book have routinely helped me immensely.

—Steve-O
entertainer, television personality, and stunt performer

Having known Jeff Kober for over thirty years, I have seen him evolve from a troubled seeker to a joyous teacher. He is my meditation teacher. Always present, he guides—with raucous laughter, humility and love. Pick any page of these 108 meditations and you will find something you needed just at that moment. As Jeff says, "It's the subtle tug of charm." Embrace the natural magic.

—Dana Delany
actor

I can't imagine starting a day without reading Jeff Kober's words. And so, every morning since I discovered his newsletter, I have had to get on my phone to read it before meditating. And every day after meditating, I have asked myself, "Why on earth can't Jeff put these in a book so that I can read his beautiful words without having to get on my phone?"

MY DREAMS HAVE BEEN ANSWERED. So have yours, even if you don't know it yet. Jeff's understanding of the Veda is matched only by his ability to articulate what we all need to hear in a way that is profound, touching, relatable and amusing. While reading his words every morning doesn't GUARANTEE an amazing day, it comes pretty damn close.

—Anna David
New York Times best-selling author of *Party Girl*

I've read Jeff's daily thoughts for years but having so many of my favorites in a collection is like having a guidebook for life. Not only does this book acknowledge the challenges we're facing, but it offers us a way to navigate through them. Jeff's words are clear and powerful, practical and joyful.

—Laura Cathcart Robbins
writer, podcaster, and author of the memoir, *STASH*

Each of these 108 pages offers a gift that one can open forever. Jeff Kober's years of spiritual exploration and teaching shine radiantly with profound transmission and practical wisdom, truly inviting the reader to be embraced by bliss. Regardless of your experience with meditation, you'll be moved and transformed by the reflections and practices contained in this gem of a book.

—Jessica Graham
author of *Good Sex: Getting Off without Checking Out*

Jeff's teachings have profoundly changed my life, allowing me to connect with something other than my thinking and live in accordance with nature. There is no greater gift. These daily reflections will touch you deeply, bring peace into your life and remind you in infinite beautiful ways, there is only one thing. And you're it! From there, what we call the miraculous becomes a part of our daily life. This book is a gift, as is Jeff! It's bliss at your fingertips.

—Ashley Hart
certified health coach, yogini, brand ambassador & TV host

I am a teacher with 30 years of experience and read your posts at my desk before I begin my work. Thank you for encouraging many thousands of people every day.

—Jen Collins Pope
secondary teacher, Sydney

Jeff Kober provides us with the best form of modern medicine— acceptance, grace, surrender, and (gasp) unconditional love. In digestible, but powerful vignettes, Kober tackles all of Life's greatest questions. He reminds us that our life is a paradox—we are both messy and perfect; we suffer and we don't have to suffer; we are human, and (most importantly) spirit. His words are steeped in an ancient universal wisdom that our body knows to be true, but that we often forget. The opportunity for healing, right here, right now, emanates from his every page. Peace now, peace now, he whispers.

—Kerry Docherty
Faherty Brand tri-founder, author of *Somewhere Right Now*

I started attending Jeff's weekly meditation meetings about a decade ago. I noticed immediately that he made the seemingly ungraspable, practical. Once he began his daily thoughts, I would hold onto them and send them to friends. I'm grateful that I can now gift them this book instead. It was a guide for me, and it will be for many others as well.

—Jordana Brewster

actor

It's rare to find a carrier of spiritual truth who possesses the ability to translate esoteric principles into practical, applicable teachings. Rarer still is the teacher with the humility to remain a student throughout their journey of awakening. With Embracing Bliss, Jeff Kober has masterfully consolidated his three decades of spiritual discovery, bridging multi-cultural concepts and timelines of non-duality and higher consciousness into a brilliant collection of digestible essays. For those who seek a message of both profound depth and simplicity, Kober has achieved a feat of great magnitude and impact for the betterment of the human collective.

—Luke Storey

spiritual teacher & host of *The Life Stylist* podcast

There's great writing—and then there's great writing that moves, inspires, heals. Kober's 108 mediations are the latter.

—Kate Atkinson

writer/producer

Table of Contents

Foreword by Rainn Wilson 1

Introduction 7

1. Following the Guidance of Nature 11

2. The Basics, Part One 16

3. Reaching from the Darkness to the Light 19

4. There is Only One Thing 21

5. I Love You, But It's None of Your Business 23

6. The Basics, Part Two 25

7. Tao Te Ching 28

8. Gandhi and the Boy Who Ate Sugar 31

9. We Put Away Childish Things 34

10. Crushed Poppies 37

11. What We Pay Attention to Grows 39

12. The Basics, Part Three 42

13. At the Mercy of Thought 44

14. Veda, Vedanta, Advaita 46

15. How Far I've Come 49

16. Asking for Help 53

17. Epitaph for Bill 55

18. Life is Difficult 58

19. How We Do Anything 60

20. All Life is Yoga..62

21. The Relative World 65

22. A Pair to Draw To 67

23. Speaking of Farming in Mexico City 70

24. You Deserve the Best 72

25. The Mind is a Brilliant Historian.......................74

26. All Life is Yoga, Part Two 76

27. Philip Marlowe and the I Ching 78

28. Maya 81

29. Your Life is Worthy of Celebration.....................83

30. Nature, God, Love, Whimsy................................85

31. Justified Anger 87

32. Like a Wave on the Ocean 90

33. I Am of the Nature of..92

34. Happiness is Only Available in the Here and Now 95

35. God is All That We Will Meet 97

36. Nobody's Perfect 99

37. Hurty-poos 101

38. Correcting the Intellect.......................................105

39. Be the River, Man...107

40. Suffering is Optional...108

41. In Death Only the Body Dies 111

42. We Cannot Hate Our Way to Love......................113

43. To See What Is 116

44. The Light of Love...118

45. The Truth of Discomfort 120

46. Personal Training 122

47. What We are is Pure Gold...............................124

48. Heaven is Within 127

49. Stop. Enough. 131

50. Dark Night of the Soul...................................133

51. Why are You Here? 135

52. Yoga 138

53. Seeking God..140

54. All We Need to Know 143

55. Stumbling Toward Ecstasy 145

56. The Power of Spiritual Intention....................147

57. The Ego as Animal 149

58. Between the Banks of Pain and Pleasure.......151

59. Compassion for the Self...................................153

60. Comfort is Overrated 155

61. The Real You 157

62. Trim Tabs 158

63. The Tracks of My Tears 160

64. Don't You Want Somebody to Love? 162

65. The Secret 165

66. Ego Was the Helper; Ego Is the Bar 167

67. Richard the Poet...169

68. Existence, Consciousness, Bliss 172

69. The Golden Age 174

70. Sometimes Life Hurts 177

71. Sadhana 179

72. The Mind Never Seems to Stop........................181

73. Trombone Playing...184

74. Sadhana Part II, or Living in the Material World...........187

75. Negative Self-Talk 190

76. Love is the Currency of the Universe 193

77. We are Made of Star-Stuff..............................195

78. Pay Attention to What Is 197

79. A Decent Regret 199

80. Thousands of Candles....................................201

81. Cosmic Consciousness 203

82. Kumbh Mela 206

83. Come to Your Senses 209

84. A Full Cup..210

85. Live Your Life Like a Prayer...........................213

86. Playing for God 215

87. Enthusiasm 218

88. Unfulfilled Expectations 220

89. Some Thoughts on Love.................................222

90. Eulogy for a Cat...224

91. To Observe Yourself without Judgment.................227

92. Dancing Back and Forth 229

93. I Love You.. 231

94. Suffering and Gratitude.................................. 234

95. A Showcase for Our Fulfillment 237

96. Free, Present, Effortless Love 240

97. The Power of a Broken Heart........................... 242

98. There is Nothing to Fear 244

99. Everyone is Capable of Evolution 246

100. Change is Inevitable 248

101. Listen 250

102. Truth 252

103. Self-Realization.. 255

104. Seva, or You Gotta Serve Somebody............... 257

105. We Cannot Hate Our Way to Love, II............ 259

106. Lifting Up the Curtain, I Have Seen 261

107. Horses 263

108. Relax and Enjoy 266

About Jeff Kober 269

Acknowledgements... 271

Bibliography... 273

Foreword
by Rainn Wilson

*"We are not human beings having a spiritual experience.
We are spiritual beings having a human experience."*

— Pierre Teilhard de Chardin

Much like Jeff Kober's daily meditations, I begin this
discussion with a quote that pretty much sums up the
entirety of life itself. When I'm feeling lost, anxious,
depressed, mired in the busy noisesome blather of daily life in big
city America, I ponder the above quote and release a sigh. Remembering, with ever deeper serenity: *"Oh, right! I am a spiritual being
having a human experience."*

This essential philosophical idea frames everything for me. It's
a 'big-picture' construct. It shifts my perspective from the frantic,
material and mundane towards a more peaceful 20,000-foot view
of the true, beautiful and still. I salute you, Father De Chardin!

This is exactly what Jeff Kober does and has been doing for
me on a daily basis since 2014. His daily email blast of Vedic
spiritual perspective has improved my days, sparked my soul and
opened my heart. For this I am so very grateful.

I don't remember exactly how his inspirational notes first
came to my in-box, but I do know that I have shared his work,
wisdom and missives with countless friends and family members.
Every single person I have recommended "Kober" to has thanked
me profusely.

"Did you read today's Kober?" We frequently say. *"Yeah, so good. Totally relate."* I frequently "steal" his awesome quotes and post them on social media, making myself look all the smarter and wiser in the doing.

Apparently, like myself, Jeff is an actor "on the side." And even though he only lives about 30 miles from me, we've exchanged emails but have never met in person. Not sure *why*. Perhaps the phrase "never meet your idols" holds true in this case. After all, if Jeff was revealed to be a big fat jerk in real life, wouldn't that forever sour my daily Kober pick-me-up?

There's a specific handful of Vedic gems of wisdom rattling around in the vast grab bag of spiritual knowledge that Jeff draws upon regularly. (Mixed with the occasional Alcoholics Anonymous, 12-step bon mot, of course!)

And please, let us note, The Vedas (which translates essentially to "wisdom") are perhaps the world's oldest "religious" texts, being chanted, gathered and written down a good thousand years before Christ. They feel ancient. And deep. And true. Undeniable in their summation of the human-divine experience in relation to the cosmos.

But what exactly is the gist of these spiritual treats that Jeff so lovingly offers up for his lucky loyal readers every single day?

From my somewhat dimwit Baha'i perspective, and from what I've read from my daily Kober, they can be broken down into five essential sections.

1. Meditation.

This is Jeff's personal foundation as well as the foundation of the Vedic Upanishads. The daily practice of devotion. Being a devotee. The spiritual act of connecting with the oneness that is in us, around us, above us, below us, before and after us. A twice-daily, 20-minute taste of timelessness. Of eternity.

I just love that word "practice." If spirituality is important to us, shouldn't it involve a practice? Some practice? I mean after all we practice our golf, piano and chess. Why not use the discipline of "practice," especially in something as simple as meditation to become ever more grounded, compassionate and connected?

2. **Consciousness.**

That's all there really is. The experience of living. The great Shakespearean Hamlet "To BE." The taking in of the sensory experience. The witnessing. Breathing in. Feeling. Noticing, connecting, pondering, remembering and *SEEING*. This consciousness vibrates, "I am." But how rarely we are truly in touch with our essential "I am-ness." How rarely we observe the miracle of ourselves simply <u>being</u>.

3. **All is One.**

Number three hearkens back to the old joke of The Buddha ordering a pizza: "Make me "<u>One With Everything</u>." All is One. There is no division. Separateness is an illusion. God, spirit, matter, identity, consciousness, time, space. All one. Sacred and profane? All one. Heaven and earth? You and me and us and them? You guessed it… ALL ONE. When we can connect with this idea, we are released from our prisons of self.

4. **The Mind and the Moment.**

There is only the now. The monkey mind wants to live in a revolving door spinning between the past and its inherent obsession—"what should have happened" and the future which keeps anxiously repeating—"I wonder what is going to happen!" Good thing the mind can be trained! As both the Buddha and that delightful Austrian spiritual imp Eckhart Tolle have reminded the modern world, "THERE IS ONLY NOW." All else is illusory. The past has already happened. The future is completely out of our control. Breathe, witness and observe the moment, the Vedic tradition and its practices implore us. So, frequently, does Kober. For in the moment, bliss and freedom await us.

5. The Ego.

When the great spiritual teacher Abdul Baha was asked over 100 years ago if he believed in Satan he replied, "Yes! Satan is the *insistent self*." I just love that. Our greatest tempter, seducer and source of evil is not some red-skinned demon living in a cave, but an ineffable force that resides within our own breasts, our own minds.

Every story needs a villain and the ego is ours. I want this. I need this. I want this outcome, this status, this accolade! I hanker and clutch and desire! That's the ever-present selfish "me" which is always fretting and declaring in its childish pomposity: "How dare they!" "Well I never!" and "Why can't I get what I want?!"

In the 12-Step tradition it's known as "self will run riot."

And this "insistent self" is running the world right now. It's literally running riot in our daily interactions, in our city streets, in our precious Mother Nature, in our media and *especially* in our government.

And that is why we need our daily Kober more than ever.

Kober provides salves and perspectives that we require both on an individual level and on a collective one. He delivers wisdom to my email in-box that specifically, in a meat and potatoes way, helps make my life better on a daily basis. And he offers Vedic breadcrumbs scattered along a path forward that, if followed, could help bring humanity to a much needed peace and understanding.

I salute you, Jeff Kober!

Introduction

For the last 35 years or so, I've made my living as an actor. I've played some dark characters—murderer, drug dealer, cult leader, demon, vampire (more than once) and Satan, just to name a few. Some people are surprised to learn that I'm also a meditation teacher. From my perspective, this makes perfect sense. In order to play with the darkness, you must be at least familiar with it. And the gift that darkness brings is the absolute need to find the light. And so, meditation.

The practice I teach comes from the Veda, an ancient set of knowledge that speaks of itself as "the science of consciousness." The Veda says that if you wish to change your experience of life, you must change your experience of consciousness.

Meditation allows us to transcend the senses, the body and even thought so that pure consciousness itself may be had. With this comes the possibility of changing and upgrading the way we look at ourselves and life so that each day we move more in the direction of our true nature, which the Veda tells us is bliss itself.

The idea of bliss is not easy for most of us to grasp, especially if we've spent years listening to the punishing voice inside our heads. It was only after decades of reading and studying with teachers further along than myself that this voice inside me slowly began to change from one of negativity to one of support.

Recognizing that it takes only a small shift each day to turn things around, I got the idea to offer the same opportunity to others—one thought each day designed to gently move the mind from despair to hope. I began writing daily Vedic thoughts for anyone who wanted to join the email list. What started as a year-long experiment has continued now for over a decade, and I have yet to find a way to stop.

These "thoughts" rather quickly became essays. It seems that either I have a lot of words that want to come out, or maybe it takes a lot of words to describe the indescribable. Perhaps both. The essays describe our world as seen through the lens of the Veda and the truths it is based on.

The Vedic philosophy of life may be stated quite simply. Something like:

- There is only one thing.
- That one thing is consciousness.
- I am. I know myself to be. To be conscious.
- Therefore, I must be that one thing.
- I am consciousness itself.

I have tried to speak to practical questions, such as: If there's only one thing, what does that mean about relationships? About work? About creativity, fear, death, despair, joy, abundance, thoughts, feelings, life, the universe, everything?

What I have gained from this experience is incalculable. Essentially, I've been putting myself through school.

Studying what?

Consciousness, awareness, life—as expressed by the great sages, the ancient rishis of the Veda, as well as modern students and teachers from a multitude of fields. I've studied consciousness as it expresses through me, in its beauty and ugliness, and by wrestling with questions posed by readers who are upset, curious or confused.

By doing this publicly, I've had no possibility of an "out." I've been here, rain or shine, sickness or health, good mood, bad mood or indifferent. I've continued learning through the years, including how to say what I know more clearly and simply. Now it seems time to put a collection of these writings together and see if they make sense as a whole.

Why 108?

In the Vedic world, 108 is a significant number. It can be found throughout nature and is used in many ancient rituals and spiritual tools.

Some say that 1 stands for God or higher Truth, 0 stands for emptiness or completeness in spiritual practice, and 8 stands for infinity or eternity.

There are 54 letters in the Sanskrit alphabet. Each has masculine and feminine, Shiva and Shakti. Fifty-four times 2 is 108.

The diameter of the Sun is 108 times the diameter of the Earth. The distance from the Sun to the Earth is 108 times the diameter of the Sun. The average distance of the Moon from the Earth is 108 times the diameter of the Moon.

If the Veda sees this number as meaningful, who am I to question a source that has been so useful to me?

I hope that reading these pieces might offer some semblance of the experience I've had in writing them so that you, too, may come to see light in the places that used to seem only dark.

Thanks for reading and for offering that reading to someone else.

Today I will notice or learn something special about the world, and I will make a point to share it.

1

Following the Guidance of Nature

One several years ago, I had some writing to do. It was a Sunday, and my son had a birthday party to attend, which gave me the perfect opportunity to get my work done. I dropped him off at his friend's house in Hancock Park, then headed to a coffee shop on Larchmont Boulevard. When I arrived, there was one table open. I got my coffee, sat down and opened my notebook.

Before my pen hit the paper, I heard my name. "Jeff, how are you?"

I looked up to see Peter, a man I'd known a little bit for a long time. Our paths crossed every few months, but in 20 years, we'd never really hung out much. Now here he was with his wife, who I'd never met. They looked so happy to see me—I couldn't help but ask them to join me, even as a voice inside of me repeated, "Please say no, please say no."

"Of course," Peter said, "We'd love to!"

So I set my pen and paper aside and settled in.

They were having a weekend-long "staycation" in Los Angeles while their 12-year-old son was studying tuba at brass camp. It was their last day together, and they were having the Larchmont experience.

For the next hour, Peter and Christie told me the story of their life together, which was really the story of their love affair. Peter was a television director, and he shared some great anecdotes about poorly behaved actors he'd met along the way. Christie had worked as an A&R rep for a major record label, and she told us about traveling through Europe with crazy funk bands and other adventures from her rock 'n' roll life. And every once in a while, they would look at each other and say, "Jeff doesn't want to hear about this. Let's talk about something else."

And then, somehow, we would just slide right back into the stories of their lives.

Now, I'd been meditating long enough to know this was about something. I put away my writing without a second thought.

"Maybe they need to learn how to meditate," I thought, even though I wasn't a teacher at the time. "Everyone needs to know how to meditate."

Then talked about a health issue Christie was having. I thought, "Maybe she needs to see our Ayurvedic doctor, Dr. Jay?" Because clearly, it was about something. I could feel that it mattered far more than anything I had planned for the day. It was fascinating, really, and by now, I was happy to sit there as long as it took.

When Christie got up to use the facilities, I said to Peter, "My God, what a delight she is. And the two of you together…"

Peter said, "Yeah, she's really something."

And then I told him, "I'm sitting here watching the two of you fall in love all over again."

And he looked at me and said, "Really, you see that?" I nodded, yes.

He said, "Because that's what I feel, too. It's so clear."

Christie came back to the table, and Peter told her what I'd said. She agreed; she was having the same experience. And the three of us sat there for the longest time, just looking into each other's eyes—free, open and alive.

Before they left, I asked Peter to speak at a gathering I was hosting the following Wednesday. He said he'd love to, so we exchanged contact information, hugged goodbye and went back to our lives.

That night, I sent him an email telling him where and when to meet. I didn't hear back from him, so Tuesday morning, I called. After several rings, a woman picked up the phone.

"Hi, is Peter there?"

And the person said, "Who is this please?"

I said, "Tell him it's Jeff. He'll know what it's about."

And she said, "One moment, please."

The phone clattered down, and after some time, Christie got on and said, "Is this Jeff?"

"Yes."

"Jeff from Sunday?"

I said, "Yeah. Jeff."

And Christie said, "He died. Can you believe it?"

"What?"

"Yesterday morning. We had that thing together on Sunday, and yesterday he went out to walk the dog, and he died!"

We spent the next 45 minutes talking—this woman I'd met just two days before. We talked about Peter, death, love and what it all might mean. She asked me to speak at the memorial service. Of course, I agreed.

I was not a teacher at the time, nor a public speaker. But I showed up and told the story of our experience together. The whole time Christie was nodding and pointing at me, telling her family, "This happened. This is what Peter and I had."

It was clear to me, and I think to everyone there, that this connection was necessary for these souls to be able to continue. Peter couldn't leave without Christie knowing how much she meant to him, and Christie had to know the truth of what she and Peter shared to help her continue on and raise their child alone.

What was required on my part was to have the sensitivity to keep my mouth closed and listen—to simply witness and reflect what I saw, heard and experienced of the two of them together.

What was needed in that moment, in effect, was an angel. I'm not saying that I was an angel. I'm saying that I got to stand in as one that day. And I was able to follow that request from nature because the voice of spirit within me was so loud that the voice of what I thought I needed didn't stand a chance.

It was one of the most profound experiences I've ever had. It required virtually nothing on my part other than to be present and offer my attention, which, as it turns out, is just about everything. This is what nature wants of us—to be available as expressions of itself and witnesses for itself. And it uses our desires and ideas of what's supposed to be happening to get us to where consciousness needs us.

Nature said to me, "You really need to do some writing," so that's what I set out to do.

Then nature had me where it needed me and made me sensitive enough to feel what must happen so I could let go of what I *thought* should happen. The result was the best possible outcome for Peter, Christie, nature and me.

Nature wants to enjoy itself and uplift itself in all ways, at all times, through each of us. When I listen for its quiet voice within, it never fails me. Nature will always show us the next right action, and when we follow its guidance, what we call the miraculous becomes a part of our daily life.

Today I will listen for the voice of guidance that comes from someplace deeper than my thinking. And I will do something that feels in alignment with that guidance, even if it makes no sense to my mind.

The Basics, Part One

It is not the facts of our life that cause us to be happy or unhappy, but rather our point of view on those facts. What may have looked like economic doom yesterday, today may appear to be completely adequate for our needs, even though our bank balance has not changed at all. We have somehow shifted out of worry and into acceptance.

Sometimes these shifts happen on their own; but we can also bring them about by doing the simple mental work required to see life through new eyes.

This is where we find the power of the paradigm we can call 'The Vedic Worldview,' which says there is only one thing, and this one thing is consciousness itself.

Some points to consider:

From the Upanishads, the ancient texts of Vedanta:
I Am That.
Thou Art That.
All This is Nothing but That.
What is That?
Consciousness.

☙

The whole of creation is consciousness.
Consciousness is all there is.

ॐ

If A equals B, and B equals C,
then A equals C.
I am, so I must be a part of the *All-That-Is*.
Consciousness is all that there is.
Therefore, I must be consciousness.

ॐ

The nature of consciousness is bliss.
The nature of *All-That-Is* is bliss.
The nature of myself must be bliss.

ॐ

What I am, in my least excited state,
is bliss.
Beyond all these thoughts and feelings,
beyond all opinions, positions, and history,
I am the place of pure bliss.

ॐ

Bliss is my nature.
Bliss is my birthright.
Bliss is my responsibility.

ॐ

If I am not feeling bliss in this moment, it is not because bliss
is unavailable.
It is because I have not yet located it.

It becomes my task then to locate it.
Here. Within the Self.
Now. In this moment.

Today I will remember that the nature of all that I am is bliss itself, and I will look for evidence of this in all my interactions with the world.

3

Reaching from the Darkness to the Light

... the question is whether the Ignorance can be transcended, whether a complete essential realisation turning the consciousness from darkness to light, from an instrument of the Ignorance seeking for Knowledge into an instrument or rather a manifestation of Knowledge proceeding to greater Knowledge, Light enlarging, heightening into greater Light, is or is not possible. My view is that this conversion is not only possible, but inevitable in the spiritual evolution of the being here.

—Sri Aurobindo
Correspondence with Sri Aurobindo

I came to spiritual seeking out of necessity and desperation. I felt like I was drowning in a darkness of grief, shame and worthlessness, and there was nothing in the world I knew that helped. Maybe in this other world of spirit, I might find an answer.

Sri Aurobindo was the first teacher who reached me in my despair and whose voice I could understand and follow. I went to India for the first time to study his work more deeply. He taught me that consciousness reaches out from the darkness toward the light, and in doing so, becomes en-lightened. And then it continues to expand for its own sake, for the sheer joy of evolving itself.

From this perspective, darkness can be seen as a gift. If I hadn't needed spiritual connection so desperately, would I have ever committed to the kind of daily work necessary to find and grow this knowledge?

Each moment of despair—or rage, shame, terror or depression—that I experience in this body triggers a story in my head that tells me I am not worthy of life. Or that the world and its problems are not worth slogging through. And each of these moments is an opportunity to turn again toward the light, no matter how hopeless it might feel that things will ever change. When we do this again and again, the light in us begins to reach out for itself, simply because that is what light does.

In the end, each one of us is here for this journey from the darkness to the light. In the infinite scheme of things, the process is already complete. The light has conquered the darkness absolutely. To remember this might make it easier to choose once more today to stay around for the joy of the journey.

Today I will remember that light is the truth of me and that whatever darkness I feel is a passing experience. I will open to feeling the light within myself and seeing it reflected in you.

4

There is Only One Thing

Dvaita: duality, duplicity, dualism
(from where we get the English word, divide)

A: not, corresponding to the English, in or un

Advaita: non-duality, that which is not divided, oneness

I have a mind that loves to complicate things. In the past, Occam's razor—the scientific principle that the simplest answer is more likely to be true than the most complex—did not appeal to me, for the most uncomplicated explanation was usually the most boring. I needed something big and grandiose to give my mind something to do other than beat me up (the thing it did best).

Since learning to meditate, all this has changed. My mind no longer needs to be kept busy; it no longer beats me up (most of the time), and simple almost always feels better than complicated.

There is nothing less complicated than the Vedic worldview, or Advaita: There only is one thing. This one thing is consciousness.

From this truth, all things may be understood. From this truth, it becomes clear that, regardless of circumstances, separation is counter to life, and unity is in support of life. I can ask myself in every situation: Am I looking to be separate from or looking to be unified with this person/situation/organization? And if the answer is "looking to be separate from," why am I here?

The Veda tells us that our job, to the best of our abilities, is to align ourselves with this truth within the relative world, where it is the most difficult to see unity. How do we do this? By loving. Love everything, all the time.

The answer to every problem is to love. The fullest expression of my deepest nature is to love. The way in which I may align myself with the flow of nature, the flow of evolution, is to love.

Simple. Not always easy, but profoundly simple.

Today I will find a way to love even that person or situation I find intolerable. And I give myself permission to love from a distance if that's what is called for. At the very least, I will find a way to move in the direction of "not hate."

I Love You,
But It's None of Your Business

If we wonder what life is about and why we are here, we can always default to the failsafe of love.

Why are we here? To learn how to love. To learn how to be loved.

What is the point of it all? Love.

What is it that, the more we give it away, the more we have it? Love.

What is it that everyone is looking to get from someone else, but that can only be felt when we feel it flow from ourselves to someone else? Love.

What is it that underpins the whole universe? Love.

If we are looking for a reason to be here, we could do worse than to choose love.

A few years back, my son and I had a bit of a falling out. We didn't speak for quite a while, at his request. It was a struggle for me. When there's a problem, I want to solve it.

Somewhere in there, though, I realized there was only a problem if I chose to see it as a problem. I realized that my job, as a parent, was to love my son. And though I didn't like it, this was the way things were going to be, at least for a while. And I began to see that loving my son did not have to look the way I thought it should look. I realized, finally, that I did not need my son's permission to love him. All I needed was my own permission to love. Without conditions, without need for anything in return.

These days, my son and I speak regularly. When he went on his first job interviews at Carnegie Mellon, I bought him a suit. He looked good. Our love today for each other looks much more the way I've always thought love is supposed to look. But it feels the same as the love I've been giving all along, with his permission and without.

Today I will choose to love someone for no other reason than because I can, and I will not ask for permission, nor will I ask for anything in return.

The Basics, Part Two

*When you know beyond all doubting that the same
life flows through all that is and you are that life,
you will love all naturally and spontaneously.*

—Sri Nisargadatta Maharaj

When we act from self-preservation, it's because we are seeing some aspect of our circumstances as threatening, to ourselves, our loved ones, our livelihood or our comfort. Sometimes this is appropriate. The fight/flight/freeze/fawn response is there to keep us safe from threat. But more often than not, we are responding to something that is merely annoying, rather than threatening, or to an assumption of threat that we have constructed within our own mind. To counteract the unnecessary survival response we can remind ourselves of the underlying reality of life that remains true, whether we are feeling it in a moment, or not.

All love is Self love, all hate is Self hate. There are no two things.

ॐ

There are those who say the unified field and consciousness are the same thing,

that everything in the universe, ourselves included,
is an expression of this unified field.
Like waves on the ocean,
we are simply waves on this
oneness of the unified field,
movements of energy through
field that are here, then gone.

⌀

The universe as we know it is infinite.
Therefore the unified field must be infinite.

⌀

Any point in an infinite field is, by definition,
the center of the field.

⌀

I am that center. You are that center.
By this definition, we occupy the same space.
How can two things occupy the same space?
It's impossible, unless there's only one thing.

⌀

There are no two things.
There is only Self.

⌀

The Self in me is the Self in you.

There is no difference.
There is only "I am."

ℋ

All love is Self love, all hate is Self hate.
There is nothing to get, there is nothing to do.

ℋ

There is only to Be.

ℋ

In meditation, we can experience
this place of Being.
Outside of meditation, in our eyes-open state,
we may assume that place of Being is present as well.
Somewhere behind
the thoughts and the feelings,
the opinions and the ideas,
Being is,
even if we're unable to feel it
in a given moment.

ℋ

We are that Be-ing now.
This truth waits only to be recognized.

Today I will ask myself: if I could be free of every idea of who I am, every idea of who I have ever been, what would I be? If I am not the sum of my history, what am I?

7

Tao Te Ching

When people see things as beautiful,
ugliness is created.
When people see things as good,
evil is created.
Being and non-being produce each other.
Difficult and easy complement each other.
Long and short define each other.
High and low oppose each other.
Fore and aft follow each other.
Therefore the Master
can act without doing anything
and teach without saying a word.
Things come her way and she does not stop them;
things leave and she lets them go.
She has without possessing,
and acts without any expectations.
When her work is done, she takes no credit.
That is why it will last forever.

—*Tao Te Ching,* by Lao-Tzu
Translated by J.H. McDonald

Some time in the year I turned 31, I had a very clear vision of a flame in the center of my chest that was just about to flicker out. Somehow I knew a part of me would die if it went out. My soul, perhaps. It scared me deeply. And so, I began to seek help of a spiritual nature. I had long since parted ways with the church I'd been raised in, and so I went elsewhere.

My first foray into Eastern thought was through the wisdom of the Chinese. The I Ching and the Tao Te Ching. The Tao Te Ching is an expression in verse form of the philosophy of Taoism, often translated as "the way."

The way toward what?

The way toward harmony with the universe. It is very Vedic in this regard: the idea that by looking, we may uncover an experience of oneness, or at least akin to oneness. "Universe" may be seen as meaning "one song," and though the term "harmony" implies at least two voices, at least they are singing in the same key.

The symbol for Taoism is the yin-yang, a circle divided by an S-curve into equal parts black and white. This represents the ever-changing nature of the universe, the flowing of life from one "way" to another. If there is a storm, it is certain to be followed by calm. Night most assuredly is followed by day. Like that. This is the gist of what I was able to ascertain early on in my reading—the only certain thing is change. I can't tell you how angry this made me.

In retrospect, I can see that I was looking for an experience of life that was free of pain, discomfort or uncertainty. I was looking for a perfection that, once attained, I could freeze in time as if I could take a Polaroid of everything just so and finally know peace. The idea that this was impossible and things would inevitably change no matter what I accomplished made me crazy. It was frightening. It made me question why I would even try. If change is the only constant, then what's the point?

When I began my study of the Veda, I found a similar idea. The Veda, too, says that change is inevitable. However, it adds something to this. The Veda says that there is only one thing going on in nature—in me—and that one thing is change. But it is progressive change. Evolution. Everything is always moving in the direction of greater wholeness, happiness and productivity, regardless of how it may appear at any given moment.

With this idea, we may learn to embrace change rather than seek some impossible perfection. We may learn to see evolution as an ally rather than the enemy. If all change is progressive change, then by definition, this next moment will be more in the direction of evolution than the moment that has just passed, regardless of how it may appear. With this as a given, my job is to recognize the progress of each moment, affirming change while at the same time letting go of all that has come before.

Change is inevitable.

All change is progressive change.

All change is for my own good, for the good of all, for the good of nature.

May I attune myself with this change now.

Today I will look for evidence of evolution in my life, even in those places my life seems to be going to hell in a handbasket.

8

Gandhi and the Boy
Who Ate Sugar

If you have a problem with sugar, don't eat sugar.

—the author

Some time ago, I was asked to write something about the intersection of spirituality and weight management. I was happy to say yes, only to watch one month, then two, go by without starting. Granted, I had been busy, but that wasn't the only reason for my avoidance. It became one of those things that niggles at the back of the brain, something you wish you'd done already, a burr under the saddle, if you will, that will guarantee an occasionally rough ride. And what is the other reason for not having written this piece? I am reminded of a story I once heard:

A woman came to see Mahatma Gandhi, waiting in line for more than half a day with her son at her side to have an audience with him. When it was finally their turn, the woman said, "Mahatma, please, tell my son he must stop eating sugar. It is ruining his health, his teeth; it affects his mood. Every time he has it, I see the change in him, and there is nothing I can do to stop him from eating it. He's a good boy, but when it comes to sugar, he becomes a liar, a thief and a cheat, and I'm afraid it will ruin his life. Please, Gandhiji, tell him to stop."

Gandhi looked at the boy for the longest time as he cowered there, trying to hide in his mother's sari. Finally, Gandhi broke the silence and said. "Come back to me in two weeks' time."

Two weeks later, the woman returned with her child and once again waited in line for hours to see the master. "Mahatma," said the mother. "We have returned. We came to you for help with this boy and eating sugar, and you asked us to come back after two weeks."

"Yes, of course I remember," said the master. "Come here, child." He motioned the boy forward.

At the prodding of his mother, the boy disentangled himself from her sari and stepped up. Gandhi reached out, put his hands on the boy's shoulders, and pulled him close.

He looked the boy squarely in the eye and said, firmly, "Don't eat sugar," then released him.

"That's it?" said the mother. "That's all you're going to say?" She was flabbergasted. "Why didn't you just tell him that two weeks ago?"

"Because," replied Gandhi, "Two weeks ago, I was still eating sugar myself."

We teach what we need to learn. I became a meditation teacher, at least in part, because I had spent so long in a constant negative experience of the world that I needed to be reminded daily of the truth of my being, the omnipresence of consciousness and the capacity of each of us for bliss. I'm not sure if Gandhi's life was improved by quitting sugar, but we know the boy was given an opportunity for change by the fact of it.

And from the Veda, we learn that everything happens for all reasons, so we can assume that whether or not Gandhi "needed" to quit eating sugar, something in his own evolution was served by the process.

So I followed his example, and at least for some time—long enough to write the piece—I didn't eat sugar. And now, more often than not, I notice when a voice other than the voice of self-love tells me to have a cookie—"Come on, just one"—and, rather than having the cookie, I can ask: "If I am not this voice, who am I? What would I not have to feel if I ate the cookie? What would I be able to continue to ignore if I ate the cookie? If I were the perfection of nature, what would I do instead?"

Today I will slow down enough to ask who's doing the talking inside my head, and I will decide if the voice is for me or against me. I will listen for the "right" thought or action to occur to me via something other than this voice.

9

We Put Away Childish Things

The demand to be loved is the greatest of all arrogant presumptions.

—Friedrich Nietzsche
Human, All Too Human

When we say we are not getting what we need from our relationship—from our partner—more often than not, we're trying to get what actually isn't available from any human. What we are seeking is available only from God.

A relationship is not a place we go to get. A relationship is a place we go to give.

For many of us, romantic relationships are where we try to work out our childhood wounds. Something missing in my life, something I should have received from my parents—love, acceptance, encouragement—that would have helped me find self-love and self-acceptance. Almost everyone we know has a version of this. We grow up never solving the equation of how to get our parents to give us this thing we needed, and then we are naturally drawn to lovers who, in some fashion, will present us with the same equation. *Maybe this time*, we think, *I'll be good enough or smart enough or something enough to get it. Finally, I will win.*

Of course, this never works out. And the chances are good that we will crash and burn at least a few relationships by blaming our partner for not doing it right. We will probably exchange these people for others because we thought they were the love of our life, but now it seems the source for fulfillment is over there. And once again, we will find ourselves in the same place with the same complaints about someone else.

If this has happened with more than one lover, we might want to look at the common denominator in the equation. That would be me. Chances are that what I am complaining about is this other person's inability to give me something that isn't their responsibility to provide. Chances are, I am demanding this other person fulfill a need in me that my parents should have fulfilled, but since it wasn't, now it can be fulfilled only by God—by my relationship to God and my inner Self, my higher Self.

A shrink once told me a story about a patient who had wanted a certain cowboy suit when he was a kid. Back then, they sold these outfits based on TV cowboys—Wyatt Earp, Roy Rogers, Hopalong Cassady, Bat Masterson. (The one I had was from *Have Gun - Will Travel*. The story of Paladin, played by Richard Boone. Black holster, long-barreled pistol, silver bullets, business cards with the silhouette of a chess knight on them. But I digress...)

This patient had asked for one of these outfits that included a vest, chaps and hat along with the holster and weapons. He thought he would get it one Christmas but didn't and carried this unmet need with him into adulthood. He grew up, started a business that became successful, and then set out to find this cowboy suit. At a certain point, a toy company went out of business, an auction was held to get rid of all the assets and this particular cowboy suit, still in its original box, came available. He won the auction, as he was willing to pay far more than the market value of the toy.

"And you know what he found, Jeff, when he got it home?" asked the shrink.

"No," I said. "What?"

"It didn't fit."

My childhood wounds cannot be healed by anyone or anything else other than me. I learn how to love and accept myself exactly as I am, and in that process, the tools I gain will help me to be most fully of service in this life. These are the gifts just waiting to be picked up by me as soon as I stop looking elsewhere to be fixed.

We embrace our wounds, vulnerabilities, and shortcomings, and together with God, meditation and whatever other sources we may find help from, and we heal. In this healing, we find ourselves able to love selflessly without expecting anything in return.

Today I will make sure I am not asking my partner to give me what can only be provided by my relationship with God. I will ask, instead: What might I give to them?

10

Crushed Poppies

To see a World in a Grain of Sand
And a Heaven in a Wild Flower,
Hold Infinity in the palm of your hand
And Eternity in an hour.

—William Blake
"Auguries of Innocence"

One day a few years back, I took a friend's photo. He wanted "something outdoors, with an out-of-focus background." We went into the backyard and pulled some lights out there. We had to go into the shadow of the next-door garage. The early afternoon sun was so strong, so high, with shallow shadows. I had him stand just on the edge of the flower bed. There wasn't much there—just some small, grassy-looking things.

We started shooting. His mother was holding a flag for my lens, but there was this one shadow on his neck.

"Hey, let's have Adele come out and hold the bounce board."

What fun that will be. Adele, her friend (and mine), our friend's son (the subject) and me. A family affair.

The day before, Adele came in from the backyard so happy. "Oh, my new poppies are coming up," she said. "You're going to just love them. We're going to have waves of orange in the yard soon."

Do you know that California poppies, before they bloom, can look like innocuous, not terribly interesting grasses?

We had crushed the poppies. Mindlessly. Unthinkingly. Adele cried.

The crushing of the poppies, it turns out, was the perfect metaphor for other things happening in her life at the moment.

We got the headshots. I felt bad. Adele wept. Then she wrote a poem about it. She'd been writing a poem every day, "Project 365," she called it. This was a particularly good one, about crushed flowers and destroyed hopes.

Making poetry out of crushed poppies—is this what it means to be human? Or what it means to be artistic? Whatever it is, it's beautiful.

To see the poetry of the crushed poppies—this is the Vedic worldview. To see the absolute beauty in all things at all times. And if we can't see it in a given moment, at least to know that it's there, somewhere, and that we will be able to see it at some point. That whatever is happening, it is always evolution. Even dead flowers are part of evolution: A heart weeps tears that need to be released. A poet writes it down. The poet's friend gets to comfort her and promise her new poppies. The poet's partner has an opportunity to be humbled and appreciate poetry and poppies in a way he perhaps never has before.

Every Night and every Morn
Some to Misery are Born.
Every Morn and every Night
Some are Born to sweet delight.
Some are Born to sweet delight,
Some are Born to Endless Night.

—William Blake
"Auguries of Innocence"

11

What We Pay Attention to Grows

Attention is the vehicle that brings our gifts to the world.

What are we studying today? What are we devoted to, busy with, concentrating on?

Left to our own devices, we are paying attention to what is wrong with our world much of the time. We're studying our problems as if thinking about challenges will help us in some fashion. We may even feel guilty if we have a problem that we're not worrying enough about.

The Veda says that consciousness is all there is. The choice we have in life is what we choose to do with our consciousness. What we do can be seen in terms of our attention and our intention.

As we learn about consciousness, we see that what we attend to grows. It's as if our attention was a magical fertilizing water hose. We go out into our garden, watering our flowers, when a small patch of weeds grabs our attention.

Oh my God, we say. Look at all these weeds. Sure, they're small now, but they're going to grow. Honey, did you see all these weeds? There must be a dozen different kinds!

And all the while, we're standing there with water saturating the weeds, giving life and fertilizer to the very things we do not want to grow. So that the next day we come out, and of course, the weeds have grown a foot overnight. And we spend even more time bemoaning our fate and this horrible blemish in our garden, paying them even more attention, ad infinitum.

This is not to say that they'll disappear if we ignore the weeds. It is, however, to say that we would be much better served by lending our attention to those parts of our garden we wish to see flourish.

Our culture has us studying acquisition, personal power, personality, self-punishment, social positioning, judgment and all other things involved in object-referral living. We are defined by how we're doing compared to the rest of the world and by the opinion of others.

As meditators, we begin to find a definition of self that has nothing to do with the outside "facts" of our life, that instead relates to what we are deep within. We at least start to understand ourselves as spiritual beings having a physical experience, rather than the other way round. We start seeing that happiness, contentment and peace may only be found through a relationship with our inner Self.

This is where we want to place our attention. We want to support the movement of our identity from object-referral to Self-referral. We do this by paying attention to what is right in our world, taking our attention out of speculation and all the "problems" that seemingly need to be solved. And we read someone else's words that support this work we are doing, even for five minutes.

Simply being reminded at least once each day that we are meant to be happy, that nature would have us be happy, has the potential to turn our day around. And if my day is turned around, it then flows out from me to affect every other soul I meet that day.

This is my responsibility. What I study becomes what I am. As a responsible citizen of consciousness, it's my job to become the best and brightest I'm capable of becoming. Why would I ever settle for anything less?

Today I will open a new book and see what it says to me. I will read something of a spiritual nature I have never read before. I will look through a book or books until I find one idea that resonates with me and I can take into the rest of my day. And when it occurs to me to worry about something wrong in my life, I will remind myself of this one concept and spend some time with it instead of with my worry.

The Basics, Part Three

The creature is in God, and God is in the creature: they
are ever distinct, yet ever united.
He Himself is the tree, the seed, and the germ.
He Himself is the flower, the fruit, and the shade.
He Himself is the sun, the light, and the lighted.
He Himself is God, creature, and Maya, (the illusion of separation).

—Kabir, from *Songs of Kabir*
Translated by Rabindranath Tagore

This universe is an observer-dependent universe.

℁

Who is the observer?

Nature is the observer.

God is the observer.

I am the observer.

℁

Attention, observation.
That which is attended to grows,
that which is observed is reflected back to the observer.

꿈

When I attend to God, my experience of God grows.
When I look for God, God is what I will find.
As I find God, God finds me.

꿈

When I observe the beauty that is the working of God in the
universe,
that beauty is reflected in me.
Reflected back and forth
—me to God, God to me, ad infinitum—
there is no limit to what may be created.

꿈

This is an observer-dependent universe. What I pay attention to
grows.

꿈

The universe is waiting for a cue from me:
What kind of universe do you want me to be?

*Today I will look for the good in everyone and everything I see, and I
will find it. And as I find the good in the world, the world will find
the good in me.*

43

13

At the Mercy of Thought

For the mind is restless, turbulent, obstinate
and very strong, O Krishna,
and to subdue it is, it seems to me,
more difficult than controlling the wind.

—*Bhagavad Gita*
Chapter VI, verse 34

Before I found a meditation that worked for me, my mind was constantly besieged with thought, as if I were in the center of a swirling chaos of voices, none of them pleasant or even remotely loving and kind. All of them spoke in one way or another of my unworthiness to be alive, and the whole of them became louder and louder over time. No matter what I did, I couldn't find any lasting relief.

The only way I could find any reprieve was to run six to eight miles a day, or smoke three and a half packs of cigarettes daily. (At times, I was doing both of these things—running and smoking—though in sequence. I never actually smoked while I ran.) Eventually, my lungs started to give out, so I had to quit smoking. My knees and back couldn't take any more running, so I had to stop that. What I really wanted was to be able to detach my head. Just take it off. That sounded like heaven to me: to be free of these thoughts, these voices of shame and blame.

Though I meditated daily (along with running and smoking), it only helped a little. I couldn't stop thinking in meditation. Sitting and watching my thoughts as a meditation, which was also a practice I tried, was just like being me, except with my eyes closed. Then I learned to meditate in this tradition from the Veda. I immediately had the amazing experience of transcending thought. My God. It was heaven. I was able to settle into an experience of consciousness other than thought, beyond thought. I was able to begin to know myself as the silence, rather than the noise I'd spent years at the mercy of. I might have wept in relief.

Nearly 20 years later, of course, I can still have irrelevant thoughts, but I almost never identify with them. The experience of quiet is there more and more, and becoming the place of self-identification, regardless of how devious and convincing the other thoughts may seem.

The more we choose silence over chatter, the less power chatter has. The less at the mercy of the chatter we become, the more we can hear the music of life ringing within the silence, patiently awaiting our attention to show us where we're needed, where we're wanted, where we are meant to be.

It's a beautiful life.

Today when I hear the voice of worry and negativity, I will choose to listen instead to the sounds of traffic outside my window, the sounds of the wind through the trees, the sound of life being lived in the city or the country, wherever I may find myself.

14

Veda, Vedanta, Advaita

Where there is creation, there is progress.
Where there is no creation, there is no progress:
know the nature of creation.

Where there is joy, there is creation.
Where there is no joy, there is no creation:
know the nature of joy.

Where there is the Infinite, there is joy.
There is no joy in the finite.

—Chandogya Upanishad

The word Veda means "knowledge" in Sanskrit. Vedanta means "the end of knowledge," or "the goal of knowledge." (Veda [knowledge] + anta [end])

The quote above comes from one of the Upanishads, the ancient texts of Vedanta. When we speak of Vedanta, we are referring to Advaita Vedanta. Advaita literally means "not two." ("A" means "the negation of," and "dvaita" means "two." A + dvaita = "that which is not two, that which has never been two.")

Advaita is a system that states that all is the Self. Consciousness. That which is me, which is you, which is the world, in the world, and transcendent of the world—all is the Self.

Toward what end do we study Advaita Vedanta, or what we might call the Vedic worldview?

Once you realize that the road is the goal and that you are always on the road, not to reach a goal, but to enjoy its beauty and its wisdom, life ceases to be a task and becomes natural and simple, in itself an ecstasy.

—Sri Nisargadatta Maharaj

We study the Vedic worldview to understand the nature of the world and ourselves in the world. We are meant to be guided by something other than our own thoughts and ideas or the ideas given to us by our culture, religion, parents, or peers. We are meant to be guided by nature itself, and nature guides us in the form of happiness.

All we want is to be happy. All our desires, whatever they may be, are the longing for happiness. Basically, we wish ourselves well... desire by itself is not wrong. It is life itself, the urge to grow in knowledge and experience. It is choices you make that are wrong. To imagine that some little thing—food, sex, power, fame—will make you happy is to deceive oneself. Only something as vast and deep as your real self can make you truly and lastingly happy.

—Sri Nisargadatta Maharaj

We study to be reminded where this "real Self" may be found, to be reminded of the only place true bliss can be found. Within.

Having never left the house, you are looking for the way home.

—Sri Nisargadatta Maharaj

It's all so very simple, and yet difficult to remember. So each day, we ask ourselves, "If I am not my thinking, then what am I? How will I be directed today? What will I use to guide me? How will I find happiness right here and now, exactly the way things are, exactly the way I am, exactly the way you are?"

Today I will choose happiness as a way of being. I will remind myself that everything I need is here, now. I will look in your eyes and see the Self and recognize it as a reflection of me. Of the Self in me. And I will open myself to the love that Self recognizes and makes possible.

15

How Far I've Come

The Creator brought into being the Game of Joy:
and from the word
Om the Creation sprang.
The earth is His joy; His joy is the sky;
His joy is the flashing of the sun and the moon;
His joy is the beginning, the middle, and the end;
His joy is eyes, darkness, and light.
Oceans and waves are His joy:
His joy the Sarasvati, the Jumna, and the Ganges.

—Kabir, from *Songs of Kabir*
Translated by Rabindranath Tagore

My first trip to India was actually a delayed honeymoon. My then-new wife was a devotee of The Mother, Mirra Alfassa, the partner and collaborator of Sri Aurobindo, one of the greatest Vedic masters of the 20th Century. Sri Aurobindo had declared Mirra to be an incarnation of the Divine Mother, the *shakti* force of nature. Indeed, she was responsible for much of what grew up around Sri Aurobindo, including the ashram in Pondicherry, South India, and the businesses and schools associated with it. The Sri Aurobindo Ashram is still there and is a thriving concern, an important stop on the South India spiritual tour for many Indians and Westerners as well.

Kelly had a teacher there, Mikael, an Israeli devotee of The Mother who taught sacred movement and practiced massage and healing in Auroville. This community outside of Pondicherry was populated by some 2000 *sadhaks* and followers of The Mother and Sri Aurobindo. We spent much of our time there with him and his best friend, Mary, an Englishwoman who was also a Tantrika. She had lived in Pondicherry for most of her adult life and was a partner on his spiritual journey.

It was just after Christmas, and the four of us were spending an evening with a man we'll call Baba. He was the head of the ashram bakery and had been there since before the passing of Sri Aurobindo in 1950. Baba was one of the foremost authorities in the world on Sri Aurobindo's 1,000-page magnum opus, a sacred poem to the Divine Mother called *Savitri*.

We read from *Savitri* and discussed it, stanza by stanza, for more than two hours, all while seated on straw mats on the cement floor of Baba's room above the bakery. The only furniture in the room was a rack where Baba hung his second change of clothes and a pad on which he slept. The straw mats were thin, and after two hours of cross-legged discussion, I was ready to move. Anywhere. My knees and my ankles were on fire. "Now, we will meditate," said Baba.

My meditation practice at the time consisted of closing my eyes and trying to still my thoughts, never terribly effective even at the best of times. So for the next 45 minutes or so, I winced and shifted as quietly as possible, trying to impress them with my spiritual commitment but feeling like an imposter. Finally bidding farewell, we took our leave and went out into the warm December evening and the quiet streets of nighttime Pondicherry. No traffic. Near silence. A cool breeze off the Bay of Bengal.

My companions all seemed to be in a state of near-rapture.

"Oh my God, that was amazing!"

"Wasn't it? I'm still floating. Literally!"

"I really felt The Mother there, didn't you?"

"Baba just radiates with her energy."

I felt like Charlie Brown in *It's the Great Pumpkin, Charlie Brown.*

"I got a candy bar!"

"I got a candied apple!"

"I got a rock."

I was the one with the rock.

Mikael finally noticed my silence. "What about you, Jeff?"

I wanted so badly to join in, but I couldn't. "Um... my knees are kinda sore."

"But what about your meditation? How was that?"

I shook my head. "Nope. Sore knees. Sore ankles. Cement floor. Straw mat. That's about it."

Much head shaking and reproach followed. I was doing it wrong. Once again.

We begin where we begin. I suppose for me, just to sit there at that time in my life was a spiritual practice in and of itself. I know that something happened that night because I remember it as if it were yesterday. I know that it was part of my path from where I was before to where I am now—it's a story I enjoy telling and a fond memory of something I shared with this woman who introduced me to the works of Sri Aurobindo, from whom I learned so much. And I know for me it's a brilliant juxtaposition when put up against my meditation practice today, which gives me so much more than sore knees each and every time I do it.

I don't believe we have to earn a spiritual practice, but in those days, I did, and this experience in Pondicherry was part of putting in my time. Thank you, Baba, Mikael, Mary. Thank you, Kelly. They were good days, weren't they?

Today I will be grateful for where I've been, for how far I've come, and for how much more there is to discover.

16

Asking for Help

I was standing in the street in Rishikesh, talking with some friends, when I felt something poke into my backside. When I turned around, I saw a Brahma bull. Fortunately, his horns were rather short and rounded on the ends, so the poke (or goose, though I imagine "gore" would be the more correct word) was probably as gentle as a bull poke could be.

I wasn't in his way. He hadn't been asking me to move, per se. When I reached out to scratch his hump, he dropped his head, nodding in pleasure. It seems he just had an itch he couldn't get to, and he picked the most bull-friendly human he could see to help him out. I was happy to oblige. It has become my fondest memory of the evening.

There are metaphors here to be spoken to, but I'm just going to go with simple and true, as I understand it:

All living creatures need each other, and we don't always know how to ask for help. So, we reach out with whatever tool we might have at hand. Some of us have nothing available but a horn.

Love is the currency of the universe. The flow of love from one of us to another feeds our spirit and fills us up. When someone reaches out to us, they most often are reaching out for love—though they may see love as a need for money or approval, apology or argument, attention or recognition in some form. They may just need a scratch in a place they can't reach themselves. No matter how they ask, it's not personal. The way they ask is a report on their own experience of life, shortcomings, and set of tools. A report on their state of consciousness. It's not a report on me. If I can remember this and not take it personally, I might have an opportunity to be of service. I might gain a return of gratitude from whatever bull has stumbled across me as a possible source of help.

And as it turns out, the feeling of giving, for fun and for free, is always better than having my own itch scratched.

Today I will try to see beyond what someone is saying or doing to see the place within them that wants only for love.

17

Epitaph for Bill

Sure, we're all going to die. But she was dying way before she had to.
I watched her fade, little by little, until 'poof,' gone.
[Hell with] that! I just want to be 'Live! Live! Live! Die!

—Overheard conversation between two former Catholic nuns

In 2016, at a family reunion in Montana, Adele and I spent a weekend taking tintype portraits of as many of my relatives as we could.

Technically, the weekend was a mess. Our first day, we got nothing; I could go into the intricacies of wet plate chemistry in the field, the absurdity of using a large brass lens on a small 8x10 field camera, and the sheer idiocy of trying to do all this in 90-degree plus weather, but I'll simply say that I was beyond happy we got any images at all that weekend.

Five of the cousins from my father's generation were at the reunion, the only ones of that age still living. We were able to wrangle four of them into the chair under the trees and make their portraits.

Bill Richter, as I recall, was my father's favorite. He would show up on the farm about once a year, often with his brother and always with a case of beer to share. What I remember about him from that time was his love of Simon and Garfunkel, especially *Sounds of Silence*. In small-town Montana, it was unheard of for a parent-aged adult to know anything about modern music, let alone enjoy it. He was one of the few who awakened me to possibilities beyond our narrow rural world.

On our second day, after nearly eight hours of shooting, I asked a cousin who was helping us out to get Bill. He was happy to come. I sat him down, set up the shot, prepared a plate and exposed it. When I put it through the chemical bath, I loved what I saw (though after the fact, I found that we could have focused one more time). Bill was standing there watching as I put the plate in the fixer bath and the image appeared (a process that always feels like magic to me).

I said, 'We nailed it!'

Bill asked, 'What does that mean, exactly?'

And I told him we got an image that captures him as good-looking as he is and is technically at least in the ballpark of okay. Bill smiled, raised his hand and we fist-bumped.

Next morning, Fourth of July, Bill and his wife went to the airport to fly back to their home in Oregon. Bill collapsed in the terminal and died.

What he had spent his time on the day before was living. Smiling. Conversing. Seeing his children and his extended family. Being with people he loved and who loved him. Being present. Sitting for a portrait. Charming Adele. And all the things one can do with the waking moments of a life. He showed that 91 can be as gracious and suave as 60, 40 or 25, and that the light we bring to life can remain undimmed right up until the moment it leaves.

It's our choice.

Today, I will ask myself: Am I in, or am I out? As Pema Chodron says, since death is certain, but the time of death is uncertain, what is the most important thing?

18

Life is Difficult

The Road Less Traveled was published in 1978, and I found it soon after. I had just moved to LA, desperate to find meaning, happiness—anything other than what I had. My life bounced between depression and despair, interrupted by occasional moments of peace brought on by just the right combination of drugs and alcohol, and the occasional experience of "falling in love." I was a mess.

Seeing me bewildered by life, someone I knew suggested the book to me, so I found my way to the Bodhi Tree Bookstore in West Hollywood and bought it. I remember getting home to my little sub-basement apartment on Highland Ave., sitting down in my salvaged-from-the-sidewalk armchair with a cigarette and a cup of coffee and cracking it open.

The first line was set apart. There it lay, thumbing its nose at me, giving me its literary finger, telling me once again, as if I hadn't heard it enough from myself and the rest of the world, that all was hopeless, nothing would ever change, and I might as well die.

Life is difficult.

I threw the book across the room. It struck the wall and then the floor, where it lay in superior smugness. Life is difficult. Screw you. I was so angry I could barely see straight. (As I mentioned, I was a bit of a mess.) So I had another cigarette, smoked a joint, had a drink, had another cigarette, and thought and thought and thought about the unfairness of this bastard world and what I was going to do now.

Eventually, I got around to reading beyond the first line and was led to the bare beginnings of a new understanding of the world, thanks at least in part to Dr. Peck's groundbreaking writings. Today I know that he was right—life is difficult and remains so until we begin to see the challenges for the opportunities they present: the chance to choose, again and again, love over separation and judgment, life over death, identity as the Self over identity as the smallness of the ego.

This is why we are in these bodies: to learn how to love; to exercise our free will, sometimes toward God and sometimes away from God; and as the teacher, David Hawkins has said, if we didn't have this world with all its challenges and opportunities for growth, we would have to build one just like it to have its gifts.

Life is difficult. Once we accept that as a given, we can move on to the good stuff.

Today I will see each "problem" as an opportunity to find compassion—for my fellows and myself. I will ask myself to love where it seems impossible to love, to accept where acceptance may feel like losing the game, to celebrate this life of possibility when it feels like there is no good option left for me to try. Amid hopelessness and despair, I will say something like, "Well, it will be interesting to see how this turns out. Help me, God, to stay present and aware and willing. Amen."

19

How We Do Anything

God may forgive your sins, but your nervous system won't.

—Anonymous

Most of us have at least something we do that doesn't fit in with who we'd like to be and how we'd like to be seen by the world, God, or our higher Self.

Maybe we secretly eat Red Vines alone at night. Flirt when perhaps we shouldn't. Lie by omission. Misstate our income at tax time. Sneak a cigarette here or there. There are oh-so-many ways to be less than we could be, than we would like to be. We think we can compartmentalize these things, turning away from the eyes of others, from the eyes of God. And from ourselves.

But how we do anything is how we do everything. We know who we are and what we've done, regardless of our capacity to deny it to ourselves. We build our lives based on what we think we deserve. And if we have secret behavior that we would judge as undeserving, it absolutely affects every aspect of our lives.

We are not aiming for perfection. As long as I am in a body, I will be subject to behaviors that might be "less than spiritual." But my point of view on myself and these behaviors can shift. I can fully own the way I behave. I can see myself and my behavior clearly. I can see myself through the eyes of the Divine with complete acceptance and forgiveness. And I can ask for help to engage in those behaviors that I would respect in myself and that are for the highest good of all.

I am a work in progress, moving ever closer to knowing myself as spirit having a human experience rather than a human struggling to connect with spirit.

So today, if I eat the Red Vines, I will enjoy them. I will stop hiding from myself. And maybe tomorrow I'll find a way to avoid eating the Red Vines, and I will enjoy that, too.

Today I will listen to the still, small voice that suggests I am better than I think myself to be. And what I choose to do today with my time and attention will reflect that better version of myself.

20

All Life is Yoga

*To find the Divine is indeed the first reason for seeking
the spiritual Truth and the spiritual life; it is the one
thing indispensable and all the rest is nothing without it.*

—Sri Aurobindo
Letters on Yoga II

Sri Aurobindo was one of the greatest proponents of Vedic knowledge of the 20th century. English educated—his father wanted him as far-removed from being "Indian" as possible—he was a scholar, author, professor, philosopher, and Indian freedom fighter. He was the first political figure to publicly call for India's independence from England, and he was arrested three times for sedition and conspiracy.

Though Sri Aurobindo was eventually acquitted of all charges, he spent a year in jail. During that time, he meditated and studied Vedic texts and, in his words, "received inner teachings on the finer points of yoga." When he emerged from jail, he was no longer interested in politics. His revolutionary zeal had been translated to the realm of the spirit.

Sri Aurobindo's writing is dense and somewhat dated—his English is exacting and precise—but it is wise and brilliant, the work of a man whose life was the laboratory for his exploration of consciousness.

I pored over his writings on my first trip to India, sometimes spending an hour on one paragraph. The books I read were just three inches by five inches, their pages filled with minuscule type. My theory was that spiritual work should be difficult.

This was my introduction to the ideas of the Veda. I had not yet learned Vedic meditation, and my intellect was the only tool I had at my disposal. I was able to follow, however slowly, the logic of Sri Aurobindo's teachings. And I was able to hear his reassurance that there was more in life than what can be seen.

There was hope, even for someone like me.

What really allowed me to trust Sri Aurobindo as a teacher was his humanness. He didn't set himself apart from others in the world. He was a man, first, and then, realizing there was more, he dedicated his life to find that something more. There are several references to Sri Aurobindo's lack of patience with students who treated him as if he had been born enlightened; that as this enlightened soul, he hadn't had to work to grow spiritually.

To this, Sri Aurobindo responded that if he had not had to work for it, it would not be worth anything as a teaching. What would he have to give if he didn't know from first-hand experience the cost of growth? How could he show others the path if he hadn't had to walk it himself?

"All life is Yoga."

This is the epitome of Sri Aurobindo's teaching. No matter what we may find ourselves doing, there is a spiritual aspect. In each situation, there is a way to practice our spiritual tools. In the teachings of Sri Aurobindo, everything is an opportunity to find God in the world; and to find God in the world is the work of life.

Today I will remember that God is in each moment. When I think of it, I will remind myself to look for evidence of this truth in the eyes of another, the words of another, in my ability to let go of my resentment or my fear or my need to control a situation.

21

The Relative World

Awareness is ever there. It need not be realized.
Open the shutter of the mind, and it will be flooded with light.

—Sri Nisargadatta Maharaj

In the physical realm, all things are relative—defined in terms of something else. Time is a measure of the revolution of the earth and its orbit around the sun, the height of a horse is measured in hands, and though light these days is spoken of in terms of lumens, not too long ago it was expressed as candle power.

Even our self-definition is relative—to our feelings and thoughts about the world, to our most recent actions or opinions, to the actions or views of others. But these are ever-shifting values. Using any of them for self-definition is like trying to weigh yourself while running—absurd and absolutely impossible to get an accurate reading. There is another way.

The *Bhagavad Gita* says, "Established in Being, perform action." Each time we meditate, we are doing exactly that: establishing ourselves in Being. Grounding ourselves in that place of "no change." With this investment of 20 minutes, twice each day, we begin to experience ourselves in a different way from a different place. We discover within ourselves an unshakeable foundation that depends on nothing in the relative world. We begin to define "self" as Self. Being. That which never changes.

When we know ourselves as that, all of life opens to us. And the relative world, rather than a place of opposites and confusion, becomes an outlet for creativity and joy where we may experience the unchanging truth of our nature, which, as it turns out, is bliss itself.

Today I will insist on knowing myself as something other than my thoughts, feelings, gender, history, opinions, job, career, bank account, closet, car, or lover. I will meditate and know that I am in contact with this other thing that I am, this place of Being. And throughout my day, I will remind myself of this and try to feel it, eyes open, in myself and the world.

22

A Pair to Draw To

It is the sand in the oyster that is the beginning of the pearl.
Fathers are a good source of sand.

—the author

One memory I have of my father is a saying he would use whenever we encountered two people—usually two men, but sometimes a couple—who looked as if they were up to no good. My father, an inveterate poker player, would nod and say, "There's a pair to draw to."

In the metaphor of poker, the pair to which he was referring would have to be seen as a low pair, deuces or treys. Fours, fives. So, in fact, they were not a pair to draw to at all. It would be best just to fold before the draw and sit the hand out. But also, there was the implication that trouble was just around the corner, drawn to the energy of the pair, and if we wanted to wait around, we could probably see it arrive.

My father lived through World War II like so many of his generation. He was mortared—his unit blown to shreds—the only survivors were himself and one other. The Army doctors had to rebuild his jaw from part of his shinbone then wire his teeth together for six months. Later in life, sitting at the kitchen table, he would sometimes cough more harshly than usual. And after minutes of the worst hacking, he would open his fist and reveal a piece of dark lead shrapnel that had worked its way through his body and had finally arrived at his lungs to be expelled.

From all reports, my father was bright, wise, loving and kind before the war. He had a great sense of humor. He was fun to drink with. The war changed a lot of that. The father I knew was more of a mystery, and stories like the one above were part of a mythology I told myself to know something about this man whose name and home I shared, but little else.

What does this have to do with consciousness? Everything has to do with consciousness. The Veda tells us that consciousness is all there is. When my father died many years ago, I had a very clear vision of him arriving at some post-body way station, no longer trapped in that packet of flesh that was my father, looking back at where he had just come from and cursing to himself: "Damn! I blew it again!" As if he was suddenly aware of the assignment he'd given himself and forgotten: to learn how to love and be loved. Understandable. It's easy to get lost here.

I spent a lot of time trying to forgive him for not being the father I thought I needed. Today this seems profoundly arrogant, that I would judge the way another expression of consciousness walked through his time on earth. Perhaps I needed to go through that process, and certainly, it's understandable; but I know now that he was the best man he knew how to be, based on the ideas he had and the tools at his disposal. And I'm sure he was the father I needed to develop the tools for life I now have at my disposal. The sand in the oyster is the beginning of the pearl. Fathers are a good source of sand.

And consciousness is a beautiful flow of evolutionary wisdom, from his father to him, to me and then to my own son, each generation taking what worked from what came before, letting go of what didn't, and remapping the path forward with each iteration.

So much of how and who we are in the world is based on the stories we tell ourselves, the mythologies of our beginnings. These days, I see my lineage as a beautiful story of success. And I mean success in the truest sense: the successive progression of life from one state to another, higher state. The movement from narrow consciousness to wider consciousness, from fragility to strength, from constraint to expansion. From suffering to joy. Had my father not suffered through his life the way he did, perhaps I would have had to suffer more on my own.

At any rate, I live my life not simply for myself but for him and every other expression of consciousness who came before us. For there is only one thing, consciousness; there is only one life, this one we are in here, in this moment. It is said that to be given life as a human is a rare and beautiful thing, that indeed, the experience of heaven itself is a body-dependent phenomenon. I am grateful today just for the chance to play.

Today I will remember my ancestors with gratitude. At a moment when I am enjoying the breeze or the warmth of the sun, I will have my father with me, in my heart, so that he may share the moment with me.

23

Speaking of Farming in Mexico City

Sometimes we speak of our meditation using the metaphor of computers. Lessons in positive thinking, for example, can be seen as new software programs. They may help, but only if we have upgraded our hardware. Cleaned up our hard drive. Our meditation and the release of stresses we get from it are the upgrades we need to run the new software programs that will change our experience of life.

A few years ago, I taught meditation to a gentleman named Gustavo in Mexico who once had a farm. Though he uses a computer now, it certainly isn't a metaphor that sings to him. Like Gustavo, I, too, grew up on a farm. When he asked me about some spiritual writings other students were talking about, I found myself saying through a translator that yes, all these books and ideas people have mentioned are wonderful, but without meditation, to study them is like planting seeds on hardpan—clay-heavy soil that, after a season of rains, seals itself like concrete. The seeds will simply lay there. And even if they do sprout, they will almost surely die.

I told him that our meditation and the release of stresses it brings is like plowing. Opening up the earth so that the seeds are accepted deep into the soil and have a chance to take root, grow and bear the fruit of a blissful life.

I saw him get it. A big smile. Maybe because it reminded him of the Bible story from his youth of a farmer scattering seeds, but mainly because it made sense, specifically for him. And for my part, I enjoyed speaking with someone who actually knows what it's like to plow—the smell of diesel and fresh-turned earth, the feel of physical labor, the trying and failing to keep a straight furrow, the joy of preparing the fields for planting, and the reward, months later, of harvesting the crop that you've loved and nurtured into its ripeness.

Today I will remember that all I am and all I have done gives me value in this world. I will insist on being present in each moment, in each encounter, so that I may pay attention to the subtle tug of charm, knowing that nature will find the way to use me, exactly as I am, for its own higher purpose.

24

You Deserve the Best

I grew up on a farm. It was easy to see that, to the cattle, the grass really does look better on the other side of the fence. The sunflowers really do follow the sun across the sky. And if I hear a dull piece of music piped into a shop and a cellist begins playing in the courtyard outside, I will leave what I'm doing to be closer to the more beautiful tones. We are always on the look out for what can improve our happiness. It is the nature of life to seek the highest experience it can discern in a given moment.

But happiness is not caused by anything outside us. True joy, the kind that stays, only comes from within. It is self-referral. If I have no relationship with my inner Self, I will never be capable of happiness.

Happiness is not something that we achieve. It is something we uncover through our inner work, through our meditation. As we let go of the stresses of our lifetime, we uncover the truth of our Being. The truth of our Being is bliss itself.

In our least-excited state, the place we touch upon in meditation, bliss is what we are. In our least-excited state, we are fulfillment. We are the source of happiness itself.

We have spent a lifetime practicing unhappiness; we will have to make the choice, again and again, to be the happiness we are. This, then, becomes our daily practice, outside of meditation: to choose joy. To choose a sense of our rightness in the world.

Guru Deva, the spiritual teacher and guru of Maharishi Mahesh Yogi, who introduced the technique of transcendence to the Western world, put it this way:

You deserve the best.
Never feel unworthy or
not justified in having the best.
I tell you, this is your heritage;
but, you have to accept it.
You have to expect it;
you have to claim it.
To do so is not demanding too much.

—Swami Brahmananda Saraswati
Shankaracharya of Jyotir Math

Today I will notice when I'm seeing the "facts" of my life as causing me unhappiness, and when I'm seeing my happiness as dependent on something that may (or may not) happen in the future. I will then choose to let go of these ideas and look for happiness in this present moment. Now.

25

The Mind is a Brilliant Historian

*We are what we think. All that we are arises with our thoughts.
With our thoughts, we make the world.*

—The Buddha (Siddhārtha Gautama)

The mind is a brilliant historian. This is its function. It can take what we've been through and describe what happened and why it happened, so that we can learn from our experiences and find a better approach for the next time.

The problem is that the mind is not always correct in its assessment. So, when we use the mind as our point of reference, as our center of identity, we can end up missing the point, the moment and an opportunity to learn. Seeing things through the lens of yesterday's experience is to miss the point of life.

We have a local market where I shop a lot. I am friendly with nearly everyone there, and on a first-name basis with some. (Recently, my son and I bought a birthday present—a very stylish hat—for one of the checkers.) But there is this one cashier. She seems shut down. Angry. Never pays enough attention to me. Doesn't allow me to charm her. At all. Won't even look at me as she checks my groceries.

This always bothered me. My mind told me every possible reason why she didn't like me. Things about myself. Things about her. None of them were very nice.

One day when I was getting groceries, the place was packed. There were big lines, except at her register. As she rang up my groceries, I noticed a passport hanging by a hook from the front of her jacket.

I found myself asking, "Excuse me. I don't mean to be intrusive, but why do you have a passport hanging from your jacket? It's so unusual."

She replied, "It reminds me [mumble, mumble]..."

"I'm sorry. What?"

"My husband died two years ago. We just went through the holidays, and when all you have are your memories, it can be pretty lonely. So this reminds me of who he was and what I had. I wear it for that."

I don't know if it helped her to have that conversation or not. I like to think it did, that sharing with someone, even a stranger, makes some things easier to bear. I know that the experience was poignant and profound for me, and not at all what I expected when I set out for cat food and bottled water. Where there had been confusion and defensiveness, there was now compassion. To me, it was one of those gems of experience that help to define one's life. It was a wake-up call that what I don't know is always much more interesting than what I think I know. When I listen to the story my mind is telling me, I miss the world around me and all the adventure and beauty available there.

Today I will consciously put aside my history and judgment of another person so that I may see her for the first time.

26

All Life is Yoga, Part Two

All life is Yoga.

—Sri Aurobindo

This is the epitome of Sri Aurobindo's teaching. No matter the situation, there is a way to practice using spiritual tools. What are "spiritual tools?"

Two things we have control over are our attention and our intention. As this separate ego that I know myself as, my attention will always be on my own needs—fulfilling my desires and trying to get rid of my fears. My intention will be to survive, get you and the world to like me, make more money, have more success, find the proper mate for tonight or a lifetime. The list is endless because there is never enough of anything, and each accomplishment leads to the need for more.

As the spirit that I am—one individual expression of the undivided whole of consciousness—my attention will always be on the world and all these other expressions of consciousness in it, with the intention to uplift, love, and come together. As spirit, knowing myself as a representative of nature itself, my job is always to be of service to the whole and ask what I might bring to a situation rather than what I need to get.

In the ego-driven example, I am self-centered—looking inward, trying to "fix" what's wrong with me and make myself comfortable and safe. In the spirit-focused case, I am centered in the Self, knowing myself as this deepest truth of being at the very core of what I am, and from there looking outward, doing my best to shine the light of consciousness into the world.

In every moment, in every interaction with another, I am serving the one or the other. I am looking at the world through the eyes of the one or the other. The spiritual work of each day— the yoga which Sri Aurobindo speaks of—is learning to choose the one and progressively let go of the other. To encourage our selves to love, randomly and arbitrarily, for no good reason. To celebrate where we can do the work of consciousness and have compassion for where we cannot.

This is the spiritual work of yoga.

And it bears noting that Sri Aurobindo, having said that "all life is Yoga," goes on to say (and I paraphrase) that if you remember this once in the morning as you start your day, and once in the evening when you end your day, this is a good day.

Today I will remember that it is my job to uplift and love everything always, and I will encourage myself to seek opportunities to do so.

27

Philip Marlowe and the I Ching

*It is only when we have the courage to face things exactly as they
are, without any self-deception or illusion, that a light will develop
out of events by which the path to success may be recognized.*

—I Ching

Without magic, there is no art.
Without art, there is no idealism.
Without idealism, there is no integrity.
Without integrity, there is nothing but production.

—Raymond Chandler

Many years ago, I studied the *I Ching*. I took a bag of books with me everywhere, and the *I Ching* was usually in the bag. There's always been safety for me in having books around; and to have a book that sometimes seems to be sentient and much wiser than me, gave me the feeling of safety on a high order.

One night, attending an acting class downtown at the Mark Taper, I left my books in the taxi I drove, and it was broken into. My *I Ching* was gone, along with my journal and books. I drove around frantically, looking in dumpsters and alleyways, hoping that the thieves had tossed out the books and just kept the leather shoulder bag, but to no avail.

A couple of months later, I was at Counterpoint Used Books in Hollywood and got involved in a conversation with a clerk there. He was middle-aged. I was in my 20s. He seemed a bit lost and almost as socially inept as I was. The reason for this became clear as he told me his story.

The book clerk was part of some obscure lineage of Jesuits, and he had spent the preceding 20 years in a monastery observing a vow of silence. The monks were allowed to speak one day each year. The rest of the time, nothing. This was the extreme he'd gone to find God.

During one of the ecumenical councils a year or two before our meeting, the church fathers determined that the vow of silence was no longer needed or even appropriate for the modern age. The Jesuit and his brothers were told to begin speaking. This caused a bit of a breakdown in my newfound friend. The foundation of his practice had been wrenched away, with nothing to replace it, and he had not yet achieved his goal of an experience of God. When we met, he had taken a leave of absence from his brotherhood and was working in this used bookstore and contemplating the idea of rejoining life and the idea of sex.

I so related to this man. He was shy and stumbling. In awe of women. His need for God was so obvious, as was his lack of direction as to where to look. These were all qualities I possessed. I began to stop in regularly. At some point, I told him about my stolen *I Ching*, and he offered his own copy. He had picked it up in his search for meaning after his silence had ended, not least because Carl Jung had written the introduction. In exchange, I gave him a first edition Raymond Chandler. Philip Marlowe. He loved mysteries. Go figure.

One day, he was gone. I have no idea where he went or whatever happened to him. I can only hope he found a spiritual practice that worked for him. But I think of him from time to time, and I can't help but wonder what he would have to say about the experience available to me each day in my meditation practice.

Any of us who look for an inner experience of God do so because we intuitively know it's there to be had. I looked for years without success. In fact, I had given up finding anything of value in spiritual practice just before I found Vedic meditation. I thought, *Maybe there's something wrong with me. Maybe I don't deserve it. God has thrown me away, and it's time I accepted my lot.* Then I learned to meditate, and it was the beginning of a transformation that continues to this day.

I think this was where my brother, the Jesuit, found himself when we met. I think he was in the process of giving up on the idea of finding God and the idea that the Divine is available within and was preparing to throw himself into the secular world with the hope he could find something of value there. For even though Philip Marlowe was never happy, at least each of his cases ended with an answer to the mystery he'd embraced.

Today I will be grateful for the mystery of life, for the idea that the answer to this mystery lies within me, and for this practice that allows me to contact this place whenever I choose to.

28

Maya

The Sanskrit term *maya* is usually translated as "illusion" and is used to describe our world and everything in it. The idea that our world is an illusion, especially to a Western mind, can be off-putting, as it seems to suggest that what happens doesn't matter. Since it's all an illusion, why should we even care about it?

As with so many Sanskrit terms, this one is often misunderstood. The central idea of Vedanta is this: There is no separation. I am at-one-with Totality. I am at-one-with all things. I am at-one-with you. With God. And yet, my senses tell me I am separate.

The life of the spirit is about seeing to what degree I can know myself as that, even when I'm having the experience of separation. When I remind myself that I am at-one-with even this co-worker who seems rude to me, it might allow me to let go of my resentment for a moment. It might allow me to see her as behaving from her discomfort rather than lashing out at me.

Maybe I'll be able to find compassion for the family member who always seems too preoccupied to pay attention to me. I might find it easier to ask a friend how they're doing, even though they rarely ask the same of me.

Remembering that I am at-one-with might help to remind me that even though I may feel disconnected from God and unworthy of God's love, neither of these ideas is even possible in a universe of at-one-with. Maybe I'll be able to stop identifying with the thoughts and feelings that tell me these things and begin to settle into the flow of life that is the truth of me. That is this oneness loving itself.

If there is only one thing, then this one thing must be God. If there is only one thing, and it is God, then I, too, must be of God. And this other person I have to interact with must also be of God. If I can even imagine for a moment that this is true, the flow of love from one of us to the other becomes possible. And where there is love, there is improvement. There is hope. There is healing.

Today I will open my mind to the idea that I am at one with another person, and I will ask myself how that might feel.

29

Your Life is Worthy of Celebration

You can search throughout the entire universe for someone who is more deserving of your love and affection than you are yourself, and that person is not to be found anywhere. You yourself, as much as anybody in the entire universe deserve your love and affection.

—The Buddha (Siddhārtha Gautama)

There was a time in my life when the only thing I seemed capable of was keeping myself alive. I required constant care and feeding from the world—cigarettes, alcohol, drugs, romance. Yet even with all that help, I could barely show up for myself, let alone for anyone else. It wasn't that I wanted to be this person who lived outside of life. I was trying as hard as possible to be here, but I had limited skills and zero belief in myself and my deserving power.

Years have passed. A deep need within has driven me to find answers that have turned around most of these former shortcomings in my life. I have let go of intoxicants of all sorts. I have become someone who shows up. I have a life that I love and enjoy. I think, in general, I am a plus in the lives of the people who know me. Who I am in the world has absolutely changed.

And yet, if I pay attention to the prosecutorial voice in my head, it's saying much the same today as it was 30 years ago. Basically, some version of *I suck, and I should die.*

I have clearly changed. The voice has not. If it were going to change based upon me changing, it would have modulated at least a bit by now; and yet that hasn't happened. Why would I ever listen to it? Just as there is not enough love, money, fame or success in the world to give me happiness, nor is there enough "good" I could be or do that would satisfy this voice of judgment in my head. Ever.

If you are a meditator and are consciously paying attention to your inner journey, you are way ahead of the majority of the world. If you are taking the time to read this, to read anything on a daily basis that's telling you something other than what the inside of your head is telling you, you are showing commitment to your soul, your higher Self. If you stop even once today and remind yourself of what a beautiful being you are and how very far you have come from whatever bottom—emotional, physical, spiritual—you may have hit in your past, then you are aligning yourself with God, Truth, and your future, which can only evolve from here.

There is no better place to be than where you are, right now, in this moment. This fact is worthy of celebration. As are you, yourself, worthy of celebration.

Today I will stop to remind myself that the voice of negativity within me knows nothing of the truth of me, or even of life itself, and I will lend myself another voice—of love, of comfort, of celebration—to point out to me the wonder of this life I have.

30

Nature, God, Love, Whimsy

*I have spent many days stringing and unstringing my
instrument while the song I came to sing remains unsung.*

—Rabindranath Tagore

There is an ancient story of a prince hunting in the woods. Spotting a majestic stag, he leaves his horse and follows the deer deep into the forest. The prince is so intent on the hunt that he loses all track of time. When he finally realizes the day is ending, he is lost. He's so far from the familiar that even if he could return to his horse before dark, he wouldn't know which way to go. As night falls, he stops in his tracks, frightened of this dark so deep that he can't even discern a path to follow.

The prince stands there, torn between this fear and his need to return. There are so many people depending on him who need his leadership. There is so much that his father has asked of him still undone. But he remains there, petrified in the dark, for one hour, then two, as the sounds of the forest grow louder and the animals inch closer, becoming bolder as the darkness thickens.

Finally, he decides to move forward. As soon as he raises his foot, a path bright as moonlight appears. He's so shocked that he pauses. And as he does, the trail disappears. Once again, the predators begin to approach until he takes another step, and the path is once again illuminated.

In this way, he is led out of the forest back to his horse. From there, free of the oppression of the woods, he returns to his kingdom and the love of his people and the meaningful life awaiting him.

What does life want from me? To ask the question is already to possess half the answer. What is the song I came to sing? I will know it only when I begin to sing. How do I find what I'm meant to be doing here? Do what comes naturally, what feels right. If nothing feels right, not even standing still, then move in the direction of your fear.

How will I know when I am headed in the right direction? When it feels good. When you lose track of time. When you can experience joy, even for a moment, in doing it.

When should I begin? Days and nights are swiftly passing. There is no time but the present. Begin today. Now.

Today I will find a reason to smile, if only for a moment, and I will ask of something greater than me—nature, God, love, whimsy, the tree outside my window—to show me a first step to take. And I will take it.

31

Justified Anger

Anger is an acid that can do more harm to the vessel in which it is stored than to anything on which it is poured.

—Mark Twain

Holding on to anger is like grasping a hot coal with the intent of throwing it at someone else; you are the one who gets burned.

—The Buddha (Siddhārtha Gautama)

Sometimes I feel like a scream looking for a mouth.

—Hubert "Cubby" Selby, Jr.

At the Sunday morning group meditation I host weekly, someone asked, "I really love this meditation. It's working. But when do I get over being angry?"

When we come to meditation, most of us have spent decades building up stresses of fear, sadness, shame, guilt, and anger that need to come out. With our very first meditation, we move in the direction of our least-excited state. From that place, nature can begin to unwind these stresses in us, the residue of all the stress responses we've accumulated in a lifetime.

As these stresses come out, we once again must sit through the discomfort of the feelings involved, for stresses coming out of our system often feel the way they did coming in. This means we experience the uncomfortable body sensations associated with these feelings as well as the urge to do something about them, whether it's fight, flee, freeze or fawn.

When we make the mistake of identifying with these sensations in our body, we think this anger is about something real. We believe it's from our present-day life rather than simply a stress leaving the body. Then we look around in our world to find its cause. And when we look, we'll always find some reason to be angry. And by finding this apparent cause, we will hold onto this stress that nature is trying to release in us.

Instead, we can name the experience "stress release." There is no cause. It is not me. It is merely a set of uncomfortable body sensations from some place and time in my past.

Then we come back to our five senses. Literally. We notice the light, shadow, colors, shapes and forms of where we are in the moment. We listen to the sounds around us. We enjoy the flavor of whatever we have tasted recently and smell the scents of our surroundings. We feel our feet on the floor, our bottom in the chair, the fabric of our shirt against our skin.

We step out of the speculation about these uncomfortable body sensations and their causes and into present moment awareness.

There's nothing else we need to do. We just let the stress go, allowing it to move through us, and reminding ourselves that we are something other than these feelings and the thoughts associated with them. We get present and move on with our day.

Yes, there is an end to the stresses that come out of us. We will reach the point when we have released all of the stresses we have spent our lives building up. Yet, even then, we still live in the world, and we will continue to have reactions to it—to the traffic, the person in line at the grocery store who is taking up our precious time, the ex-spouse.

Each of these reactions will cause their own chemical swirls within us, their own stresses, but as meditators now, they won't stick, and we will simply release them as well.

This is the way nature works—evolving us, making us whole, clearing away everything that stands in the way of our usefulness to the world and our ability to love. Nature needs us to be fully here, free and alive. And as we meditate, it will take care of the details.

Then it's our job outside of meditation to move toward joy at every opportunity and away from anger, resentment, fear and despair. We choose, again and again, to be here, be present and let nature take care of the rest.

Today I will choose to let go of any anger I am holding, even if it's justified. I will choose to be present in the world. I will choose to be open to experiencing the joy of living.

32

Like a Wave on the Ocean

Love says, 'I am everything.' Wisdom says, 'I am nothing.'
Between these two my life flows.

—Sri Nisargadatta Maharaj

Who am I? Am I this body? These thoughts? This packet of desires? Am I the religion I practice? The money I make? The gender I am? The opinions I have about life, about you, about myself, about anything? Am I the opinions you have about me?

The Veda says that I am the whole of nature having an individual experience. Like a wave on the ocean. There is no point at which the ocean ceases being ocean and becomes a wave. The wave is absolutely, completely ocean—curved ocean. Nothing more. Nothing less.

Like this, I am nature. All else that I am—the thoughts, feelings, opinions—is something to be set aside in order to experience the truth of what I am. The nature that I am.

Twice each day, we sit in meditation and de-excite this wave function that we are in order to feel the oceanic Self that we are. We align ourselves with nature. And as we do so, more and more, we become the expression of nature we are meant to be.

Today I will remind myself that I am something more than my thoughts, feelings and opinions. I will ask myself: who is it that experiences these things?

33

I Am of the Nature of

I am of the nature of Absolute Existence,
Absolute Consciousness, and Absolute Bliss.

—Sri Adi Shankaracharya
Nirvana Shatakam

S ri Adi Shankara, the teacher who reinvigorated the study of the Veda in India in the early 9th century, did something that had never been done before. He brought the teachings of the Veda to the common people, sharing the Upanishads with them.

The Upanishads are recognized as the culmination of the knowledge of the Veda. The main point of the Upanishads is summed up in this sloka (verse):

"I Am That.
Thou Art That.
All This is Nothing but That."

There is only one thing. And everything is of that one thing.

This had always been secret knowledge. Why? Because if "I Am" is the truth, what use will I have for priests or temples or rulers? If all of us are That, why should I be your servant? Why should I allow you to remain in power?

The ruling classes didn't want to lose their power, so they kept the truth from their workers. Sri Adi Shankara changed all that.

He brought to the common people the truth of their souls, thus beginning a revolution in consciousness that utterly transformed the land of India.

In the quote above, Sri Adi Shankara says, "I am this ultimate reality. Existence, consciousness, bliss." He doesn't say "we" are this thing because he speaks from his identity with the Oneness. He is speaking out for us as the Oneness. He is shining a light until we, too, are ready to have our own realization of this truth.

If there is only one thing, there is nothing to harm me. If there is only one thing, I must be that one thing. If I am that one thing, I have nothing to fear, for fear requires a sense of other.

And if there is only one thing, even God need not be called upon, but simply opened up to; for again, if there is only one thing, then even God must be closer to me than my own breath. And if this is so, then there is absolutely nothing outside my capacity to have, realize, access, embody.

Even the gods, powerful as they may be, cannot prevail against him, the man who has known Brahman (Oneness).

—Adi Shankaracharya,
commentary on the Brihadaranyaka Upanishad

Sri Adi Shankaracharya lived for only 32 years, some 1200 years ago, and yet today, his words still have the power to redirect, transform and heal, for they are the truth.

Today I will hold gratitude in my heart for all those men and women who, through the ages, have offered themselves as beacons, guiding us toward the Truth of our Being. And I will remind myself that everyone I know is seeking a beacon of their own, a way out of fear; and perhaps as I live today in gratitude and loving-kindness, I may be a faint version of that beacon for someone else.

34

Happiness is Only Available in the Here and Now

Studies show that people are thinking about something other than what they're doing nearly half the time. This mind-wandering is composed of regret—imagining what we could have done in the past to make things come out better—or speculating about how to behave in some future experience. The studies also show that these imaginings always result in less happiness.

We can't ever actually be anywhere but in the present moment. No one has ever revisited the past or stepped into the future. We are here, always. Trying to manage our past and future experiences to find greater happiness in this here and now has never worked, nor can it ever work. *Thinking* in the past or future is not the same as *being* in the past or future.

And no matter how well we may "figure things out," our speculating mind does nothing, ever, to change what has happened or what will happen. Placing our awareness in the future or past takes us away from the only place we ever might find happiness—right here, right now.

We have been trained by life and our neurochemistry to worry about what's ahead of us and feel guilty about what's behind us— automatically shifting our awareness out of the present and away from where we are. But simply by becoming aware of this habit and then insisting on coming back again and again to where we are, what we are doing and how it feels to be in this body, the happiness that is the baseline of the universe—*Sat-Chit-Ananda* (existence, consciousness, bliss)—becomes available to us. The Veda says this bliss is the truth of all that is. I am part of all that is, so this bliss is also the truth of me.

In this moment, right here and now, happiness is available. Always. We only need to step out of our thinking to look for it where it lives.

Today I will insist on being present at least twice, or at least five times, or as many times as I might think of it: as I am tying my shoes, walking from the car to the house, putting on my jacket, brushing my teeth, pouring my orange juice, doing sit-ups or asking my friend how she's doing.

35

God is All That We Will Meet

On whatever path people walk, they come unto me.
Whatever form or aspect of mine they worship,
Toward that very aspect I strengthen their faith;
And through that faith they come unto me.

—*Bhagavad Gita*
Chapter IV, verse 11; Chapter VII, verses 21-22

The *Bhagavad Gita*, one of the ancient Vedic texts, speaks of the oneness of the universe. All that seems separate from the whole—myself, my dog, this computer, everyone on Facebook, jihadists, their victims, the Blue State politicians, the Red State politicians—is simply a unique expression of this one complete thing. Like waves upon the ocean: each different in size, shape, intensity, duration, rising up and seemingly separate, yet still pure ocean, through and through.

There is only one thing. I am this one thing. As are you. As is everyone.

The Veda also speaks of the existence of the Divine, the reality of God in "whatever form or aspect" He/She/It may be worshipped, sought or recognized. There is acceptance of the absolute Truth of the existence of God.

There is only one thing. I am this one thing. As are you. As is everyone. As is God.

It doesn't matter what path we walk, we will meet God. In fact, it might be better to say that no matter what path we walk, God is all that we will meet, ever. In the trees, the flowers, the breeze upon our faces. In the smiles of the people who welcome us, in the rolled eyes and judgment of the people who don't. And in the faces of all those so busy with their own troubles and thoughts, they don't even notice we are here.

There is only one thing. God is. Where in this equation can we find room for God not to be in these people at this moment, no matter what?

The only question then becomes: *Am I willing to look for God, no matter what?* No matter what kind of day I've had, how much money I owe, how many buckets of problems I carry; and no matter the challenging nature of what others might bring my way, and the opinions and judgments that arise within me as they behave so humanly.

Am I willing to look for God no matter what? The Veda tells me that if I am willing, I will find what I'm looking for.

Today I will look for God in each moment, in each face, in each encounter, no matter what. And I will let myself off the hook for those moments when I find this impossible to do, knowing that I, too, am this one thing.

36

Nobody's Perfect

Out of the crooked timber of humanity,
no straight thing was ever made.

—Immanuel Kant
Idea for a Universal History
with a Cosmopolitan Purpose

P erfection is not possible in the relative world.
The word perfection means "completed." So by definition, if you're still alive, it's not possible to be perfect.

We want our teachers to be perfect. But our teachers, all of
them, are human. Some would say "flawed." But the proper term
is "human." One more man or woman moving from birth to
death, and in that passage, learning to love and be loved. Some are
enlightened in a broad sense, some more narrowly. The best of
them allow their humanity and don't spend time trying to appear
to be something they are not. They fall down somehow, then they
stand up and make corrections, using their experience as a part of
their teaching from then on.

I dated a spiritual teacher briefly back when I was quite a bit
less than refined as a human. To some, I was seen as a "bad boy"—
attractive enough and charming enough, but guaranteed to be
trouble, if not today, then soon.

This teacher used to tell the story, "Once, in Hugo's Restaurant, I was introduced to a man by a mutual friend, and as he was leaning across the table, shaking my hand, I had the very clear image flash through my mind of a railroad crossing, red lights flashing and the arms coming down. What do you think I did?"

The answer, of course, was when I asked her out, she said yes. Then, after the inevitable happened and I showed myself to be a less than stellar romantic partner, she found herself with this story to tell by way of illustrating her humanness and her ability to take the lesson offered and move on.

And now I get to use the story, too, to illustrate my own brand of character shortcoming and offer myself as an example of someone who can see himself truly, take responsibility for the less than stellar behavior, and change. (This person and I are friends these days with nothing but respect and love for each other.)

This is perfection. The perfection of a human proving themselves utterly human while moving toward the ideal of the utterly Divine, and in full acceptance of the mess and the beauty that path implies.

Today I will take time to see myself as filled with the Divine and forgive myself for not always knowing it.

37

Hurty-poos

A man is standing on a street corner, weeping. His best friend and
business partner has run off with his wife, his kids, his dog.
The IRS has taken his business. In the midst of all this, his house
burns down. He's lost everything. He looks to the heavens and, in a
pleading voice, says, "Lord, why me?" And from out of the skies above
comes a rumbling voice that says, "I don't know, George.
There's just something about you that pisses me off."

—Traditional

Sometimes we will take life and the people who populate it
personally. No matter how aware we might like to think we
are, no matter how far we have moved toward a more
spiritual approach to life, there are times when we will get the
hurty-poos.

What are the hurty-poos? Self-pity, feeling like a victim. *Why*
me, Lord? These would be the hurty-poos.

As meditators, we have an assignment to let go of expectations.
On a daily basis, we remind ourselves there is something going on
here that is bigger than me. Yes, we have thoughts, feelings,
opinions, ideas, a body, a self-image, but who we are at the core is
something other than any of these things and greater than all of
these things together. To embrace this idea and feel this deeper
thing in meditation, we become able to notice that most of our
"negative" thoughts and feelings are simply the experience of

releasing stresses from the body. Knowing this, we can let them go and move on, feeling lighter, better about ourselves, and more at peace with what is.

Then there are those times when someone really does treat us badly, is disrespectful, scares us, talks behind our back, ignores us, cheats us, cheats on us, or even worse. At those times, we are legitimately victims. We have been "victimized." Something has happened to us that would not have happened in a "fair" universe.

And our mind sets out to make sense of it all: Nobody loves me. I've always been alone. I'll always be alone. Life is a tragedy. Love doesn't exist. God hates me. This world is a vale of tears. I am not worthy of life, love, or happiness. On and on…

None of this is true. Most of these thoughts are simply programs that have been instilled in us by family, church, the French existentialists, our chosen peer group. They have been triggered by our circumstance—and by the feelings of stress release that occur whenever we are triggered into a negative experience of life—and we are left at their effect.

So, we use terms like "hurty-poos" to wake ourselves up and remind ourselves that:

1. We are having "uncomfortable body sensations." This is not betrayal, fear, anger or hatred. To name these feelings is to try to get some control over them so I can make them go away. The opposite is true. When I name them and resist them, I keep them around. My job is to accept what is—all these sensations—without insisting they all have a handle.

2. These sensations and the negative thoughts our mind floats to us to explain them are evidence of stresses being released from our body. Stresses that may have been caused by the

hurty-poo incident itself, as well as every other experience we ever have had that is echoed by the incident, stresses that we perhaps have been carrying for decades. When we recognize this phenomenon and label the thoughts and feelings appropriately as stress release, we can let them go, surrender them to the ethers, come to present moment awareness and involve ourselves in the healing flow of life.

3. We must stay out of speculation and the suffering it brings. There is nothing to figure out. There is nothing to fix. As meditators, there is only the need to let them go.

4. With those around us, regardless of how wronged we may have been, we try to mind our manners and not act out our discomfort on others (for example, our spouse, who has been sitting patiently beside us for hours on a road trip).

5. When we find we have been unable to fully mind our manners, we make amends with as much grace and alacrity as is possible (for example, buying said spouse a set of jade earrings in some romantic, out-of-the-way artist's studio alongside a country road).

6. We remind ourselves that this, too, shall pass: the hurty-poos, the seeming lack of grace we may be exhibiting, the minor bruises we inflict on the ones closest to us, the exhaustion of "feeling too much" and trying to "process," the unstressing, the letting go. All of this is ephemeral, momentary, gone almost before we know it.

Today I will notice when my thoughts and feelings are telling me that I am a bust, that the world is a bust, and I will remind myself this is evidence of stresses being released. This is not a report on any truth of my life. And I will get present.

38

Correcting the Intellect

Meditating twice daily will change your experience of life, absolutely, but to transform your life, you have to include the practice of "correcting the intellect"— building a new model of the universe to affect your understanding of life.

All things in nature seek happiness, or well-being, in one form or another. My Labradoodle snuggles next to me because it gives him pleasure. I let him because it gives me pleasure. Sunflowers follow the sun across the sky because it is their nature to have as much light as possible. We seek happiness because it's in our nature to do so. But we've been trained to look outside ourselves for happiness, in spite of the fact that it's not available in the outer world. The teachings of non-duality suggest a different way of seeing.

The Veda says that consciousness is primary. The implication is that my experience of life is based not on the so-called facts of my life, these outer experiences, but on my interpretation of those facts.

For example, if I feel unhappy, I may think my unhappiness is because I don't have enough money. One approach to my problem is to make more money. *How much is enough to achieve happiness? Who knows? We'll just have to see. What yardstick should I use?* If I've never had enough money, it will be hard to come up with a way of measuring. All I'll have to go on is my level of happiness.

I may think I'm unhappy because I don't have enough money, but what if that's only a partial truth? What if I also have unfulfilled experiences of creativity, relationships, health? What if my unhappiness is biochemical and related to eating sugar, flour or dairy? To drinking? What if I just wake up each day with a reset button of low-grade misery? If any of these issues are a part of the equation of my lack of fulfillment, I can make money from now till doomsday and never find lasting happiness.

So, we correct the intellect. We begin to teach ourselves that happiness lies within. We study a philosophy of life that shows us how happiness is not dependent on anything outside the Self. We become aware of our thinking and call a timeout when we find ourselves veering into self-pity, blame and complaint.

We ask ourselves: What would life be like if Totality was nothing but consciousness? What if consciousness and God were the same thing? If Totality was everything and everyone, all the time—including me, right now? What if God, consciousness and I were inseparable? What if my happiness depended solely on my continued decision to be happy?

Today I will ask the universe: What kind of life do you want me to have? And I will assume that the answer includes happiness and that this happiness is available within me now.

39

Be the River, Man

Human life is like the bubble that appears in the stream.
You see it one moment and then, the next moment, it is gone.

—Sri M

One of the interesting things about human life is the shift from our early experience of time and how it might drag on and on—*How long till Christmas? When's Daddy getting home?*—to the experience of our later years when the days and years flow by like bubbles on a stream.

The truth, from the perspective of infinite spirit, is the latter. We are here and then gone. The bubbles rise and disappear in a moment as the stream goes on and on. If all I am is the bubble, this is a sad state of affairs. If, however, I am the stream, the coming and going of bubbles is just part of the joy of living, of flowing.

Meditate today. Be the beautiful evanescent bubble you are but know yourself as the stream. Or as my dear friend Diana is fond of saying, "Be the river, man!"

40

Suffering is Optional

Pain is physical; suffering is mental. Beyond the mind there is no suffering. Pain is merely a signal that the body is in danger and requires attention. Similarly, suffering warns us that the structure of memories and habits, which we call the person, is threatened by loss or change. Pain is essential for the survival of the body, but none compels you to suffer. Suffering is due entirely to clinging or resisting; it is a sign of our unwillingness to move on, to flow with life.

—Sri Nisargadatta Maharaj

The existence of suffering is the great, unsolved problem of the modern world. So many people suffer, and so few systems, religious or secular, offer relief. Many of the world's religions actually teach that suffering is a virtue—not because the benefit of suffering is plain to see, but rather because no one can tell you how to avoid it. It's here. We've all experienced it. What does it mean?

In the Vedic worldview, it's clear that suffering is not a given. Instead, it's founded entirely on our point of view on the facts of our life. To the precise degree that I am unable to find acceptance of some aspect of my life, I will suffer. Though I may continue to feel discomfort, I will know peace to the degree I can find acceptance.

Looking at it in this way, suffering is a choice. I want things to be a certain way. Things turn out differently. I am unable to let go of my want, and so I begin to speculate:

What does it all mean?

Why me? or Why not me?

What if I had done this thing differently?

What if I hadn't said that thing?

What if I had waited? What if I had gone sooner?

What if I had prayed harder?

Why didn't I _____?

If only I had _____?

Is there something wrong with me? With them? With the world?

Does God hate me? Is this happening because I hate God?

On and on, we live in our past and replay it so that maybe it will come out differently, or live in a future where things turn out the way they should have, or where I die because I screwed up so badly, in every case, not living at all in the present. Missing out on my life. And suffering.

In meditation, we discover the truth of our Being: that beyond our small self—our thoughts, ego, self-image, history—we are perfect, whole and complete. We are exactly who and what we are meant to be, now, in this moment, and everything is exactly as it is meant to be, now, in this moment. Without exception. Tragedy, comedy, like it or not.

It's up to me to accept this, not begrudgingly, but with the joy of knowing that I am aligning myself with Self by accepting my life exactly as it is. With nature. God. And by this alignment, I am finally making myself available to the support that Self/nature/God has been waiting to give me.

Today I will let go of the idea of how things should be in my life. I will get present to what is, and I will accept it exactly as it is—fully, completely, joyfully.

41

In Death Only the Body Dies

In death only the body dies. Life does not, consciousness does not,
reality does not. And the life is never so alive as after death.

What was born must die. Only the unborn is deathless.
Find what is it that never sleeps and never wakes,
and whose pale reflection is our sense of 'I.'

—Sri Nisargadatta Maharaj
I Am That

In the Vedic worldview, death is not the opposite of life. It is,
rather, an integral and essential aspect of life. And to
understand life, we must understand the truth of death.

The long and the short of it is this: There is something that
does not die when the body dies. This something is consciousness.
It is what we are. "I" do not die. This body dies, this mind dies,
this ability to experience the physical realm dies, but I go on.

Our body is dying all the time. Cells are replaced continually.
It is said by some scientists that there is no cell in my body much
more than a couple of years old, including my bones and teeth.
Yet "'I' remember being a 5-year-old, an 8-year-old and a 12-year-
old. I remember being 40 and 50. Obviously, what remembers is
not the body.

What is it?

It is consciousness.

The Veda says that consciousness is all there is.

I am. This much I know. And according to the Veda, this "I Am" is consciousness. Before this body was born, consciousness was. When this body fails, consciousness will continue.

We meditate to introduce ourselves to this "I Am." We go beyond our thoughts, feelings and ideas, and our experience of this body to begin to know ourselves as something "other than" all this. We meditate to know our true Self. In a very real sense, when we meditate, we are practicing dying. We are going beyond all these ideas of self to an experience of Self. And rather than being frightening or painful, it is pleasant, profound and quite often fun. It is an infusion of life. It is the supremely comforting experience of that which never changes, which never dies, which goes on no matter what happens here at the physical level. Like finding your true tribe, at last, you belong.

Today I will imagine what life would feel like if I could be free of suffering, trepidation and the fear of death. I will ask myself to imagine joy everlasting, and I will seek to feel some small part of it in my day.

42

We Cannot Hate
Our Way to Love

We cannot hate our way to love.
We cannot kill our way to fearlessness.

We are not humans seeking a spiritual experience, but rather spirit having a human experience.

What is the human experience? It is the survival pyramid of the animal nature and the stories we tell ourselves to make sense of it all.

The animal nature seeks survival of the self, first, survival of the herd, second, and comfort, third. The stories are what we identify as: I am black/brown/white, straight/gay, woman/man /nonbinary, citizen/alien, red state/blue state, right/more right.

The survival system triggers us into fight/flight/freeze/fawn, and we behave from these deep animal directives. Why am I so angry? Whose fault is it? Why am I afraid? Who's causing it? Do I have a right to be angry? What can I do to make it go away? What does it mean about me that I'm afraid? What does it mean about the world? Where can I run? Who can I fight?

The word for all this is "ego."

Spirit having a human experience is the soul taking form as this human nature, forgetting itself, again and again, becoming lost in the humanness of self constantly, and continuously remembering/reminding itself that it is spirit. Spirit watches the ebb and flow of needs, wants and desires, the nearly constant triggering of fight/flight/freeze/fawn, and steps back from it, disidentifies with it, and lets it flow through the system without taking it so personally or being driven by its demands.

When we live solely identified as the ego in the relative world, we feel the solution for the fear, pain and lack of safety must be found in the relative world. Some people seek it in banding together, finding safety with their own kind. Others seek the answer by making enough money or having enough power to be safe on their own, to find happiness in their own small part of the world. And still others seek the solution by determining who the enemy is, then plotting how to get rid of them. Send them back. Put them in camps. Let them starve. Keep them out of our part of town. Kill them.

When we live in the realm of spirit, we know the world as one whole complete thing and ourselves as at-one-with that. We know that fear and anger are the energies of the physical nature and do not define us, do not have to be listened to. We know that as the oneness of life, it is not possible to hurt you without hurting me, that you love your neighbor as yourself because your neighbor *is* yourself. We know that love, though not always felt, must always be sought and that love is exponentially more powerful than hate. We know that raising our own consciousness, filling ourselves with love, elevates the consciousness of the whole, brings love to all. A rising tide raises all ships.

We cannot hate our way to love, but perhaps we can love our way through a day and begin the process of healing that our world so desperately needs.

If consciousness is only one thing, then what I do in consciousness affects the whole of consciousness. Today I will take the time to settle past all the negative voices in meditation and then offer the love and peace I find there to my world.

43

To See What Is

Be where your feet are.

—Anonymous

O ne of the greatest misuses of our energy is speculation. We look to the past and imagine what should have happened that would have led to happiness now. And we look to the future, conjuring up what needs to happen now for us to find happiness there. Most of our "problems" are based on these negative assessments, comparing the "what is" of life to the "what should be" and assigning blame for the distance between the two. *If only I weren't so lazy. If only she hadn't done that thing. If only I'd had different parents. If only I could get that job/lover/check in the mail.*

Speculation leads only to unhappiness.

Our job each day is to see what is and find our place within it. This means to be present to the world and other people in it, rather than to our thoughts, feelings and opinions about it.

When we step out of the constant chatter of blame and negative speculation and into the flow of life, we become able to call upon the true Self that is always there, just behind the thoughts. And if we take even a moment to listen for the silence behind the rattling of the mind, we send a message to the whole of the universe that we are interested in joining the flow of it, rather than trying to "figure out" our little corner of it. We give permission to the whole of this universe to guide us and work through us. By surrendering the false control of worry and blame, we begin to discover what's actually happening and what wants to happen to us and through us.

And what is it that's actually happening? Love. The universe is in the business of coming together with itself, through you and me and all these little moments of our lives. It is about enjoying itself right here, right now. It is about giving itself, through me, and you, permission simply to be.

Today, when I find myself beset by worry, I will give myself permission to be fully present, just for one minute—not trying to shut off the chattering mind, but simply paying attention to something or someone else. The sound of a dog barking, the half-smile of a new mother with her infant in the park, the feel of the baking sun on the skin of my arm, and the cool breeze of the evening when the sun goes down.

44

The Light of Love

There the sky is filled with music:
There it rains nectar:
There the harp-strings jingle, and there the drums beat.
What a secret splendour is there, in the mansion of the sky!
There no mention is made of the rising and the setting of the sun;
In the ocean of manifestation, which is the light of love,
day and night are felt to be one.
Joy for ever, no sorrow,—no struggle!

—Kabir, from *Songs of Kabir*
Translated by Rabindranath Tagore

One way to enlightenment? Love. Love everything, all the time. This is what psychiatrist and spiritual teacher David Hawkins advises. This is what the great saints of the world show us by their actions. Love God. Love the world. Love God in the world. Love everything.

The Veda teaches that God is all that is. Everything is of God—literally made from God Itself. It may not be easy to see this God, but It is there in everything, waiting for us to notice; and as we learn to love, it is God we are loving. And it is God (within) from which we love. We can begin with the easier things: dogs, babies, our favorite sister or brother. Milkshakes, thunderstorms, the handsome man laughing with his friends, the beautiful woman touching her cheek as she contemplates her day.

And then we can move on to the more challenging: traffic and nosy neighbors, physical work in the cold and wet, the self-obsessed cell-phone-texting-in-the-middle-of-the-aisle-at-Whole-Foods man or woman who won't let us through, who doesn't even notice we are there, who couldn't care less. Love them. Then you've built a muscle. Then you're starting to recognize God.

Love as an idea does nothing but sit there waiting for something worthy of it, waiting for The One. Love as an action steps out and looks for a place to connect, one indication of worthwhileness. Love as a tool for enlightenment flows and always is looking for an outlet, a target. Continuously looking for evidence of God, insisting it is there to be found. And insisting that love is the answer, the key, the one right thing. Always.

Today I will find something or someone to love, just for a moment. In that one thing or one person, I will look for just one aspect that could indicate the presence of God. And then I will find something else or someone else to love, just to see if I can keep it going.

45

The Truth of Discomfort

Ask the physicist. He'll tell you: 'It's all mere vibration; particles or charges in constant motion or just waves of different frequencies in a perpetual flux. Your three-dimensional world is largely a concoction of your senses and mind.' And you? You are the consciousness which is the witness of all the drama, watching in amusement as the ego plays its games, dons different masks at different times and ends up identifying itself with the roles it plays. The real you is that ever-blissful, unchanging, blessed consciousness.

—Sri M
The Little Guide to Greater Glory and a Happier Life

When I was in India on the Walk of Hope, each day was a new experience of discomfort. Blisters upon blisters, shoes that didn't fit, heatstroke. Too-spicy food and cold showers. Dormitory sleeping quarters. Dust and smoke, not knowing Hindi, away from family and friends. The list could go on.

But ask me how my experience was, and I'll tell you it was fantastic.

How is that possible?

As Sri M says in the passage above, I am the witness to the drama, witness to the discomfort. I am not the drama; I am not the discomfort. The discomfort was a given. The source of it and the intensity of it changed on a day-to-day basis, but I never for a moment entertained the notion I could be comfortable. And because I meditate twice each day, I can remember that part of Self that is the witness. I'm always just a few hours away from the experience that reminds me of this Truth of Self.

This is the gift of meditation: the ability to go beyond all that seems to be "wrong" in the world to touch upon and identify as that which is absolutely "right," always. This is not to say that the happenings in the world are an illusion. The challenges we all are facing in these difficult times are absolutely real. But the more I know myself as that which is beyond my troubles, the less I am at the mercy of my problems, and the more of myself I can commit to changing what needs to be changed in my world.

Today I will meditate twice, morning and evening. During the hours of the day I am not meditating, I will remember the Truth of what I am, reminding myself that the underlying Truth of me IS, and always will be, regardless of my outer circumstances. To know myself as this underlying Truth is to be able to call on the power of consciousness itself and bring it to bear on what must be changed in my world.

46

Personal Training

Live in the sunshine, swim the sea, drink the wild air.

—Ralph Waldo Emerson

Sometimes I work with Maria, a personal trainer. She's amazing. She takes you right to the edge of working too hard, but never over, and without it feeling like you're killing yourself doing it.

Maria is one of my heroes. A couple of years ago, I watched her prepare for a triathlon. Biking, running, swimming. Now, doing a triathlon, whoever you are, is pretty amazing. But Maria didn't swim. At least not until a couple of months before the competition. Then, she learned. Now, she's an ocean swimmer.

One day she said, "You know why I'm doing a triathlon? Because this is the stuff I'm the worst at. I can do the strength training kinda thing all day. But this... this takes work. I'm not good at this, so I'll just make myself compete at it."

That's why she's my hero. This is how to embrace the idea of success. Success is not winning, but rather, progressively, day-by-day, fulfilling more and more of our potential.

Once, Maria and I got together after a two-week break. I hadn't done a lot of work in the interim, and I was disappointed with how much I could do in our session.

Maria said, "But you did 100%, didn't you?"

"Yes," I said.

"Well, that's what we do. 100%."

"But it was off from last time," I said.

"Don't compare to last time. You gave 100%. But your 100% changes. That's what matters."

Today I will give 100% of myself to something.

47

What We are is Pure Gold

Truth, like gold, is to be obtained not by its growth,
but by washing away from it all that is not gold.

—Leo Tolstoy

The Veda says that we are spirit. We are not this body, this mind, these thoughts, feelings and opinions. We are this other thing, this deeper thing: Spirit, nature, totality. By any name we call it, we are this oneness with each other, with all that is, whether we can feel it or not—and this oneness supersedes all differences.

What good does it do for us to see ourselves this way? Let's say you're at work. You've spent days on a project doing your best, following the protocols established by your boss and team. Now that the groundwork has been laid, a co-worker is assigned to the project with you.

After looking things over, he says in a snappish tone, "Why did you do it this way?!"

Suddenly, your hackles are up. You want to snap back—your mind fills with images of hurting him. But you're a spiritual person. You hold back and answer as calmly as possible, "Because that's the way we discussed doing it." And then you turn and walk away before something in you flies out without your permission.

Now, your body is aflame with the swirl and spin of uncomfortable body sensations—shame/anger/hurt/rage. Your mind is running with all the thoughts brought about by these feelings: *What's wrong with me that someone speaks to me like that? Who does he think he is? Why didn't I read him the riot act? What a wimp I am. Why does the world keep doing this to me?*

If I am my thoughts, feelings and all these body sensations, then I'll have to figure out the answers to these questions and resolve the situation with this other person (who may or may not want to resolve it with me). And, I will be uncomfortable, and my head will be filled with negative speculation till this resolution occurs.

If, however, I am other than all this—if I have come to know myself as Self, as spirit—then I can see these thoughts, feelings and uncomfortable body sensations as mere stress release: the release from my body of the stresses that have been stored there by every other life experience I've had that's even remotely like this one. This experience allows me to let go of all of it—all that's in me that is not gold.

We still will feel uncomfortable. But we will be able to remember that the feelings will come to an end. They will leave the body. We will discover that our endless speculation about the meaning of the feelings and the interaction itself keeps the feelings alive in us.

When we stop feeding the process with our attention, all the discomfort naturally flows through us, leaving less stress to carry around. We'll be left with the knowledge that next time we have an interaction like this, we will have less of a reaction. Maybe we won't take his tone personally. And by not taking it personally, we might be able to see that our co-worker spoke to us not to shame us but because he was frightened in the moment that he would not be able to do his job. With less of a reaction, we might be able to reassure him that it's all going to be okay, that together we'll be able to solve whatever problem he's feeling overwhelmed by.

What we are is pure gold, and our journey here on the planet is to let go of all that is covering up this truth.

Today when I feel drawn out of the moment of my life and into speculation about what all these uncomfortable feelings mean—about myself and the world—I will remind myself that I am pure spirit. And to remember myself as spirit is all I need to do to begin letting go of this swirl and spin and get back to the business of life.

48

Heaven is Within

*The 'kingdom of Heaven' is a condition of the heart—not
something that comes 'upon the earth' or 'after death.'*

—Friedrich Nietzsche
The Antichrist

A friend of mine used to say, "Imagine the most beautiful
spot you can: in a meadow, next to a burbling mountain
stream, cool, soft grass to lie on, sweetly scented breeze,
butterflies flitting all around. The nearby peaks are glistening in
the sun. All of it is as if nature had decided to give you the most
ideal day imaginable. Even at your most cynical, to be dropped
into this paradise would take away your darkness immediately.
You couldn't help but fall in love with life, let go of every negative
thought and dark impulse, set aside every unresolved issue. In spite
of yourself, you would have to relax and enjoy your experience.

"Got the image? Good. Now, imagine being there for
eternity."

Suddenly, what seemed like heaven would become a pretty
good descriptor of hell.

A 2005 ABC poll found that 89% of Americans believed in
heaven as a place one goes after death—where either one is without a body, or where one's body is restored to perfection. This is
a very Christian perspective, yet this idea does not align with what

Jesus says in the Bible. In the Gospel of Luke, Jesus is asked by the Pharisees when the kingdom of God will come, the Jewish people of that time expecting a Messiah who would bring his kingdom to the earth:

And when he was demanded of the Pharisees, when the kingdom of God should come, he answered them and said, 'The kingdom of God cometh not with observation: Neither shall they say, Lo here! or, lo there! for, behold, the kingdom of God is within you.'

—Luke 17:20-21
King James Bible

The Gospel According to Thomas is a first century non-canonical text which was found in upper Egypt in 1945. It was one of the Gnostic Gospels that the Church ordered destroyed as Christianity worked to define itself in the years after the death of Jesus. Some scholars believe it was written by those who actually knew Jesus, as opposed to the authors of the four gospels we know. In this text, the message of Jesus is even more clear:

Jesus said, 'If those who lead you say to you, 'See, the kingdom is in the sky,' then the birds of the sky will precede you. If they say to you, 'It is in the sea,' then the fish will precede you. Rather, the kingdom is inside of you, and it is outside of you. When you come to know yourselves, then you will become known, and you will realize that it is you who are the sons of the living father. But if you will not know yourselves, you dwell in poverty and it is you who are that poverty.'

—The Gospel According to Thomas, verse 3
Translated by Thomas O. Lambdin

This is the Christian idea of heaven stated clearly by the central figure around which the religion was formed. Why then isn't it a part of traditional mainstream thought and belief?

I think it has to do with suffering and the fact that no one knows what to do with it. Without an examined life, without a way to know oneself as something other than one's thoughts and feelings, we are at the mercy of the mind. We are subject to the speculation that leads to suffering. When even the leaders of a religion are unable to relieve their own suffering, let alone that of their congregants, they must come up with a vision of heaven that is somewhere else. Because if it exists here and they can't find it, what use are they? And if it *doesn't* exist, why bother at all?

Heaven exists. It is, as Jesus says, "inside of you and outside of you." And how do we find our way to this experience of heaven? In the following line, He tells us: *"When you come to know yourselves, then you will become known, and you will realize that it is you who are the sons of the living father."* By knowing ourselves. By going within and knowing ourselves. As we do in meditation.

This is our task: to sit in meditation, twice daily, in order to let go of the stresses that keep us from feeling and seeing paradise; and then insist daily that we find the way to love despite everything that tells us not to. We have to find a way to enjoy ourselves no matter how much grief is in our lives, and find a way to open ourselves up to the experience of life more and more each day. Because if heaven is here, then it must include everything that's here, so a good start would be to stop ignoring and start loving, everyone and everything, ourselves included. No matter what.

Today I will seek to love at least one person, perhaps from afar, whom I find it challenging to love. And I will insist on at least one moment of enjoyment— a fast car or a hummingbird or a baby's smile or a good apple—and I will allow for the possibility of finding heaven on earth.

49

Stop. Enough.

Somewhere around the age of 48, I stopped trying to fix myself.

For most of my life, I felt I was broken, that something was terribly wrong with me that had to be healed before I could be happy, know peace and have a life worth living. I can trace the brokenness to a life-changing trauma in my teens. From that moment on, I felt outside humanity, unworthy of life and love.

For more than 30 years, I tried to repair myself, first by using any substance or behavior I could find to numb the pain; and when that stopped working, reading through the spiritual libraries of the world, trying to get "better." Some things worked a little. Some worked a little more. Some worked not at all. I studied, I learned. I traveled to India. I visited priests and therapists, holy men and holy women. I changed. I grew. But still, there was a wound in me that wouldn't heal. It could be soothed for a moment with success or with love, but it never went away.

One day I found myself thinking, "Stop. Enough. This is it. This is your life. You're done. If it hasn't happened by now, it's not going to happen. If it hasn't changed by now, it will never change. You've got about 70% of yourself back. That's going to have to be enough. 70% is quite a bit. Be happy with that."

And I quit trying to get better.

About six weeks later, I learned Vedic Meditation. From that moment forward, I have become more and more what I've always wanted to be, which is simply awake, aware and present; happy, joyous and free; able to love and to be loved; and useful on the planet exactly as I am, bruises and traumas included.

A year after learning the meditation, I remembered the 70% conversation I'd had with myself. And I found it was no longer true. I was beyond 70%, maybe even 100%. I no longer felt broken, and I could see that, in truth, I had never actually *been* broken. I'd always been whole but had never been shown how to know that wholeness. Now someone, something, had shown me, and I was able to own it for myself.

We find this formula throughout the spiritual literature of the world—someone struggles and fights toward a goal, then finally gives up; and in the giving up, something happens. We can suddenly take our place in the world and discover who and what we are, rather than trying desperately to become something or someone else. In giving up, we allow ourselves to be led by something other than our egos. And the seemingly miraculous ensues.

There is nothing to achieve. There is nothing to be other than what one is. There is nothing to become. We are what we are, as God made us. Beautiful beyond measure. When we find the way to feel this, we can begin to accept it. And accepting this truth of what we are, life can begin. This can happen today. It can happen in this moment.

Today I will ask myself what keeps me from accepting myself and my life exactly as I am. What part of me am I unwilling to accept? What would happen if I stopped trying to fix everything and just tried to get along with who I am? Is it possible to feel at peace, to know joy and to give of myself exactly as I am right now, today, in this moment? If there were a God, and God was all-loving, is there anything I am that this God would not, could not love? If the answer is "no," then who am I to say differently?

50

Dark Night of the Soul

It is only by our endless fumbling through darkness
that we make ourselves willing to reach for the light.

When I learned Vedic meditation, from the very first session I knew I had found something different. Finally, a practice that worked for me.

As I went forward with my twice-daily meditations, I found that the practice continued to be effective. Each time I meditated, I became just a bit freer of the ego and its difficulties. I went beyond thought and feelings. Consciousness expanded, drifted or dove into the deepest levels of Being. And after 20 minutes, I emerged feeling peaceful, sometimes blissful, and always deeply rested. This has not changed. Over 19 years later, I still have experiences each time I meditate that I wouldn't trade for anything.

But after a while, I began to notice that, on another level, I was disappointed. I expected meditation would render me perfect in some way. I hoped it would take away my pain and suffering and keep me from ever experiencing the darkness I used to live in. I imagined it would cure me of my "character defects," so I would no longer be at the mercy of the ego's neediness and its unending manufacture of fear.

This was not the case.

The ego has not gone anywhere. Fear-based behaviors do not change overnight. Habits of a lifetime are not always so easily set aside. However …

Life does become infinitely more pleasant, acts of loving-kindness easier to choose. We begin to identify more and more with the deeper Self rather than with the ego. And at those times when the darkness and the demons do arise—which they will—we can trust we are experiencing them because they are being released. Our twice-daily practice dissolves the stresses we've been carrying for ages. All we need to do is continue forward, remembering the truth of our Being despite all thoughts, sensations or ideas to the contrary:

- God is all there is.
- The Infinite All has been created out of the very stuff of God.
- We are made of this very stuff of God.
- As such, we can't possibly be what the darkness might say we are.

What we are, always, is pure, perfect, whole and complete. And as these stresses dissolve and unwind from our body, this perfection of Being begins to shine within as the truth of us.

It is sometimes uncomfortable, this letting go of the negative and laundering of the stresses. Still, for each moment of discomfort, there is a corresponding awakening of our ability to know joy. A good exchange, and well worth it, always.

Today I will recognize the negative voice of stress release, and I will refuse to believe what it says about me or the world. And even though I may not be able to feel it in the moment, I will remember the truth of my Being and my oneness with the Divine.

51

Why are You Here?

The secret to life is meaningless unless you discover it yourself.

—W. Somerset Maugham
Of Human Bondage

For years before I learned Vedic meditation, I looked for a spiritual path that could work for me. I stumbled forward, trying things on my own. Even going to India the first few times consisted mainly of reading books and attempting, with little success, to quiet my mind.

I did take one meditation class in the early '80s. It was with a Buddhist monk from Thailand, every Tuesday night for six weeks in West Los Angeles. There were 15 or 20 students. He showed us how to breathe, sit and place attention on various parts of the body. I loved the way he talked about consciousness, and I did experience some peace in his presence.

One night, toward the end of our time together, he went around the room. With each person, he asked a question, made an observation and/or touched them gently. And in every case, the student either burst into tears, sobbing in that soul-clearing way that can indicate the beginnings of true transformation, or broke into peals of laughter, infecting all those around them—again indicating a major shift.

It was beautiful.

From my place in the back of the room, I watched with awe, gratitude, anticipation and a bit of trepidation because, at that time, I believed I wasn't worthy of anything loving and kind. I thought I was different somehow. I felt separate and apart from them, and I was afraid I'd miss what the others were experiencing. Still, I held out hope.

With only a few of us left to go, the little monk stopped in front of me. He took my hands and cocked his head, gazing at me quizzically for the longest time. The room fell silent. Finally he said, "Why are you here?"

Oh, no. This wasn't at all like the questions he'd asked the others. I tried to answer, stumbling over the words. "Um... to learn to meditate?"

He smiled and shook his head as if to say "come on," then asked me again. "No. Why are you here?"

Oh, God. My stomach dropped. I felt the beginnings of anxiety creeping up the back of my neck. "Uh, because... I... I want to learn how to meditate?"

The monk stared right at me. He let go of my hands. "Why are you here?" Now he was stern.

I had no idea what answer he wanted. I tried to start a sentence, "I... uh..." but I had nowhere to go with it, so I just shook my head. *Tell me!* I wanted to say. *Why am I here? Maybe that's why I'm here—so you can tell me why I'm here!*

But the little monk just dropped his gaze, shook his head again, somewhat sadly, and moved on to the other few people still left. I had missed my chance. For healing. For release. For relief. Though he stared at me a few times in the final sessions, the monk never spoke to me again, and I never figured out what he was asking or how I was supposed to have responded.

To the enlightened mind, there is no space; there is no time. There is only the Here and Now. Totality. Though he asked the question then, the answer I have today comes from my current understanding. Now I like to think the monk was asking me the big question: "Why are we here? Any of us? All of us?"

To be enlightened, of course, would be the answer. To find God. To know Totality. Or, to put it in more human terms: to learn how to love.

These are reasons to be alive. I imagine that my answer to the monk from here at the far end of the telescope is meeting his question there in the past. He is smiling and nodding at me with the approval and love I so desperately wanted then. And from the place I am today, I can smile and nod back at him and say, "Thank you. Good class."

Today I will know that I have a purpose, and that it will become apparent simply by virtue of my continuing to be open to the question and by asking myself, whenever I think of it, how might I be more loving?

52

Yoga

Yoga, the act of yoking, joining, attaching, harnessing, putting to (of horses); a yoke, team, vehicle, conveyance.

—Sir M. Monier-Williams
A Sanskrit-English Dictionary

Yoga is the joining of one thing to another.

Here in the West, the word is generally used in reference to hatha yoga, the physical practices set forth by Patanjali and now developed into the countless schools of yoga we find everywhere, some with a "spiritual" aspect, others concerned mostly with yoga as a form of exercise.

In truth, yoga, in all Vedic references to it, is about the joining of individuality to universality. As Monier-Williams further states in his definition, "...its chief aim being to teach the means by which the human spirit may attain complete union with... the Supreme Spirit." This is true for hatha yoga and for all the other forms of yoga referenced in the Veda. All are avenues by which the student seeks "union with."

Dhyana yoga, or meditation, is one of the paths presented by Patanjali and referenced in countless Vedic texts; but it is only one. There is also the yoga of action or work, *karma yoga*; the yoga of knowledge, *jnana yoga*; the yoga of love or devotion to God, *bhakti yoga*; and others.

The Veda is concerned with the attainment of union with this thing that is greater than oneself. And whether we call it nature or God, Oneness or *Ishwara*, everything that we do, and the spirit in which we do it, move us closer or farther away from this union.

So, at each moment, we might ask ourselves the question: Is this action/thought/behavior moving me toward God or away from God? As meditators, the answer will be there. Always. Then the question becomes, "if it is not moving me toward God, do I still wish to be involved in it?"

We will find that some days the answer will be no, some days yes, and others it will be "I don't care." And given that everything is about movement toward this union, we will begin to know that even the days of "I don't care" may be used by nature to help us on our journey.

Today I will find at least one thing to do that unmistakably is a movement toward union with something greater than myself. And I will let myself off the hook for the things I may do that are not in the direction of that union.

53

Seeking God

Are you looking for me? I am in the next seat.
My shoulder is against yours.
When you really look for me, you will see me instantly—
you will find me in the tiniest house of time.
Kabir says: Student, tell me, what is God?
He is the breath inside the breath.

—Kabir

During the winter of 2013, I traveled with a small group to Maha Kumbh Mela. This once-every-12-year gathering of holy men and women and spiritual devotees is in Prayag, one of the most sacred places in India. It attracts 100 million people over the course of six weeks.

One evening while wandering through the madness, we were approached by a group of four or five young Indian men. This happens a lot in India. Young men stop you—to ask questions, to have their picture taken with you, to take your picture, to practice their English on you, to flirt with the Western women. This time, the young man shook my hand and smiled.

"Hello. Excuse me, sir. May I ask you a question?"

"Of course."

"Where you are from?"

"U.S. Los Angeles."

"Very good. U.S.A."

Indians, by and large, seem to love the U.S.A. Perhaps a rarity in the world. We do have democracy in common—theirs is the largest in the world, ours one of the oldest.

The young man continued:

"How are you liking India?"

"I am liking it very much."

'This is good. Good. Tell me, sir. What do you find is the biggest difference between your country and mine?"

"In my country, we have forgotten about God. Very few are seeking God. But here…"

I gestured around us, to the 20 or 30 million there at that moment, making a pilgrimage to this place to seek connection to something greater than themselves. The man smiled, radiant. I had given him an answer he liked.

"Yes. This is true, sir. Everyone here is finding God. And you are here."

"Yes. We are here. It's beautiful."

"It is beautiful. Yes. Thank you, sir. Hari om."

"Hari om. Thank you."

Beyond all else, this is the difference between Indian culture and our own. Yes, people there are seeking happiness. They are looking to make money, be successful, have family, find love. But also, to a large degree, the people of India believe in a divine presence in this world, and they see a loving connection with it as a prerequisite to happiness and fulfillment. Connection to God first, and then business. God first, then family and love.

Here in our culture, the default approach to happiness often seems to be to seek money and success first, and then if there is time left over, maybe seek God. Or maybe not. To seek relationship, but as a place to find fulfillment, rather than as a place where we might fulfill our responsibilities of love and family in a God-centric world view.

And what we find is that the Indian people seem by and large happier than our own. More welcoming. More open and accepting. "You are here at Kumbh Mela, respecting our traditions and seeking what we, too, are seeking. You are welcome."

This is not to say there is no seeking of God in our culture, but rather that our searching is done on a much smaller scale: One person, one prayer, one congregation, prayer circle or group meditation at a time.

But this is not a given. We don't need to go to India to change things. We can ask ourselves the questions here: What would it be like to feel God in the world? To see the truly devout everywhere you turned? To find all religions and spiritual approaches acceptable? To seek evidence of God in the eyes of a stranger and see in those eyes that the stranger is seeking God in you? Not just at Kumbh Mela, but in the East Village; on Ventura Blvd. or Melrose Ave; in Billings, Montana or Mexico City; in the coffee shop, the workplace, the supermarket or across your dining room table?

Today I will seek a way of seeing the world that shows me something larger than myself, greater than my ideas, grander than my hopes and dreams. I will seek an experience of love, of God, with everyone I meet, and I will stay open so that my fellows might find an experience of God through me.

54

All We Need to Know

God resides in the heart of every person at every moment.
He is always ready to take care of you.
Develop your spiritual powers.
This is true knowledge.
And to apply oneself to His service is true devotion.

—Guru Deva
Swami Brahmananda Saraswati

The spark of the divine is in each one of us.

—Sri M

This is all we need to know. To know God, to find God, we need only to look within our own heart. To know how we are to treat others, we need only remember that within each of us is this same divine spark.

To know how we are to be in the world, we need simply to remind ourselves that service is the key and that what we are serving, always, is either the ego or God.

In each moment we may choose to find God within, and to serve God in the world. This is all we need to know. After this, all the rest is simply the joy of discovery.

Today I will find God within my own heart and know for myself absolutely that I may find God in you if I choose to look.

55

Stumbling Toward Ecstasy

By your stumbling, the world is perfected.

—Sri Aurobindo

Each of us arrives on this planet without knowing how to live. We must be taught to sleep through the night, walk, use the toilet, speak, and ask for what we want. We must be taught to share, read, listen, and learn. And all the time, we are also figuring out how to be a daughter or son, brother or sister, friend or enemy. How to be a student or teacher, how to grieve, how to celebrate. How to give love. How to make love. How to accept love. How to let go with love.

The whole of life is on-the-job training. Not one of us arrives here knowing how to do or be any of these things. Even if we believe in past lives, the "how" of living does not carry over. So, we learn how to do everything as we're doing it. We don't take classes in digging a ditch. We pick up a shovel.

We don't take classes in falling in love. We simply stumble across an experience of someone that causes a download of bliss chemistry. And then we stumble toward this other person and, if their chemistry causes them to stumble in our direction, we stumble together. Then we fumble or stumble our way through a kiss, date, relationship, marriage. We feel our way forward, each moment new (whether it feels novel or not), each moment there to be discovered (whether we think we know what we're doing or not). And we learn.

How do we learn? By trying and failing. By making mistakes. By doing it the way that feels natural, or the way we've seen it done by others—our parents, peers, teachers—or by doing it the opposite of the way we've seen it done. We try it one way and fail. Then we try it another way, and perhaps fail a little less.

To be human is to mess up, again and again. To be spirit is to know that this falling and rising is how we move toward the Divine. We are grand, exciting, growing, living, failing creatures. And if we find we are not making mistakes, perhaps it's time to try something new.

Today I will accept my fallibility and that of my loved ones. I will let myself off the hook for my mistakes, knowing that I am an expression of life itself, which always is doing the best it knows how to do, in all its myriad expressions; and knowing that tomorrow, having learned from my mistakes of today, I will be able to do it differently, and perhaps even more successfully.

56

The Power of
Spiritual Intention

The search for happiness and meaning in our life can feel overwhelming. So many things to manage: our job, politics, the global pandemic, finances, relationships, business relationships. Then there's the health of our children, parents, spouses, and ourselves. We try to arrange things to find happiness, and we're rarely successful. As soon as we get one area of life "solved," another needs our attention. We find the "right" partner, but we need to make more money. We make enough money, but we need to find more fulfillment in our work. The goalposts keep moving.

Then at some point, we become interested in spirit. Perhaps we are drawn by curiosity. Perhaps we have a friend or relative whom we've seen change and grow because of spiritual work they are doing, and we'd like some of that in our own lives. Or perhaps we become so overwhelmed, so beaten down, that we see no way out other than a miracle. A spiritual solution might look like our only chance.

Our starting point doesn't matter. What does matter is the day-to-day choice to continue. Continue meditating, studying, practicing our dependence on something deeper than what exists on the surface of our lives. As we do so, we may find things become more manageable. We may stop trying to change the facts of our life and try instead to change our point of view on those facts. Instead of living solely in the world of accomplishment and accumulation, we meditate to spend time in the place of pure Being where we can find peace and the feeling that everything is perfect exactly as it is. We may begin to know that our commitment to spiritual growth is the single most powerful thing we can do for ourselves and the world. By growing our own consciousness, we affect not only everyone around us but also the consciousness of the whole.

As the Veda says, consciousness is all there is. What any one of us does in consciousness affects what every one of us experiences in consciousness. Knowing this, we want to ask ourselves, "What am I bringing to consciousness today?"

Today when I find myself with options, I will choose to feed the spiritual rather than the relative. I will choose to grow my connection to the realm of the Divine rather than to the world of objects and sensations. And I will choose to see those around me as my brothers and sisters rather than as my competition.

57

The Ego as Animal

D avid Hawkins, the spiritual teacher, tells the story of putting a teddy bear in the passenger seat of his truck. He called it "Ego." When another driver got in their way, he would turn to the bear, pat it on the head and say, "You're right. They *should* die. They cut us off. Good boy."

The ego's job is to judge, to keep score. It does it whether we give it permission or not. Living from the amygdala, it receives information from our senses before our forebrain does, reacting to the world before we have an opportunity to choose an appropriate way of being.

The ego sees only separation. It sees us always as one-up or one-down, and it catalogs all the ways we are better than or worse than. And for every one of these uninvited flashes through our mind, we judge ourselves. Continually. This can be hell.

Most of the people I know are involved in self-improvement. They read spiritual books, meditate, practice yoga, try to eat well, go to the gym, go to therapy, take classes, sit in 12-step groups. Many of them practice some form of daily self-examination— checking their behavior as much as possible to see that they are not behaving from selfish motives; noticing where they have been cruel or judgmental and then trying to make things right; amending their behavior.

For some, this push for perfection seems like a full-time job. And almost without exception, these same people live with a harsh inner critic who rarely acknowledges growth but instead points out every imagined transgression; or projects that same judgment out onto the world.

It is a spiritual truism that everyone is always doing their best. This includes me, right now. This includes you, right now. We are worthy of life, love, and joy. We are here in this life for a reason, and we are meant to live in such a way as to discover that reason. We do this by moving in the direction of life and permission, rather than in the direction of death and judgment; by knowing ourselves as worthy of love, rather than deserving of hate; and by being aware in each moment of our day that we are not this animal nature, but rather what lies behind it.

We are not these adverse reactions to ourselves and the world, but rather a force of love and light. We let the negative chatter run its course, but we cease listening to it or taking its assessment of us as valid in any way.

What we are is beautiful beyond measure. And this world, too, despite its hardships and ugliness, is beautiful beyond measure. Each moment of this life is a gift. For us to remain sitting in judgment of ourselves or anyone else is to refuse this gift.

How sad is that?

Today, when I find myself listening to the voice of the inner critic, I will thank it for sharing and then redirect my attention to the world around me. When the voice tells me something negative about someone else, I will look at them for evidence of their lovability. For evidence that person too, is a child of God, worthy of every good thing.

58

Between the Banks of Pain and Pleasure

Between the banks of pain and pleasure the river of life flows.
It is only when the mind refuses to flow with life, and gets stuck at
the banks, that it becomes a problem. By flowing with life I mean
acceptance—letting come what comes and go what goes. Desire not,
fear not, observe the actual, as and when it happens, for you are not
what happens, you are to whom it happens. Ultimately even the
observer you are not. You are the ultimate potentiality of which the
all-embracing consciousness is the manifestation and expression.

—Sri Nisargadatta Maharaj
I Am That

If I am the ego, then I am identified by every "good" thing I know about myself, and every "bad" thing I know about myself; or by the way I feel—pleasure or pain—at any given moment. These qualities change constantly, and my point of view on some of them can change on a daily basis. And if what is "good" or "bad" about me is determined at all by the people around me, these things will change each time I move from one conversation to another.

This is way too much work. One of the great gifts of being on a spiritual path is that we can begin to identify as something other than the ego. Whether or not the voice of the ego is chattering away at me, telling me I am better than or less than someone else, that I am good or not good; it means nothing to me. If I know myself to be the Self that is true, that underlies all my thoughts and feelings, and all the chattering of the mind.

Even on those days when it might seem impossible to know myself as anything other than my problems, those days when "spirituality" is the furthest thing from what might feel real to me, I can remind myself that in meditation, I can have the experience of dropping in and transcending this surface experience of self. I can sink into a deep, quiet, boundlessness where I am able to feel at peace. And I can remember that there are those who say this unboundedness is what I truly am.

Even as a possibility, knowing this can be enough for us to release our attachment to the pleasure or pain of a moment, which in turn allows us to rejoin the flow of life. By joining the flow of life, the relative problems will work themselves out more often than not—sometimes with our help, but often without any input us at all.

We are here to be alive, to enjoy life. To enjoy freedom. As Sri Nisargadatta Maharaj says elsewhere, "Freedom is letting go."

Today I will let go of those definitions I hold of myself that keep me from my life. I will refuse to listen to the voices of negative self-judgment. I will do one thing today that is not something "a guy/gal like me" would do. And I will enjoy it.

59

Compassion for the Self

Imagine a compassion large enough to encompass even yourself.

—Dr. Tony Cahill

How does compassion for the self feel?

Imagine watching a 4-year-old working alongside her mother in the kitchen. The mother is making cookies. The little girl, standing on a footstool, is making her own batch. Imagine her making the biggest mess possible, dough and flour everywhere, all over herself and the counter, in her hair from where she's had to move it out of her eyes. She's not making the mess just to make a mess. She's making a mess because that's what 4-year-olds do when they try to do an adult task.

Watching this, we would be charmed. We might be impressed by her commitment to this thing that is so obviously over her head. And if the cookies got baked, we would probably eat them and enjoy them, making sure the little girl knew how much we appreciated the work she did to make them.

Now imagine an all-loving Creator, watching his creations move through life, evolving with each moment, situation, and day; always stepping into new situations and challenges; for indeed, each day is unique. We are evolving creatures, designed to continue learning, always needing a new level of skill, a fresh way of seeing things, a novel approach. Always reaching for something more, sometimes succeeding, and other times failing—occasionally, spectacularly so. That Creator probably would feel about his creations how we feel about the little girl.

This is a model for how we might feel if we could imagine a compassion so big that it is not just for others. A compassion for ourselves.

Each of us is always doing the best we can at any given moment. We can look at who we are today and see how much we have grown from five years ago, from ten years ago. We can see how much more capable we are, how much more we can love. Yet, we're still self-critical. We talk negatively to ourselves. We berate ourselves for our shortcomings. What level of success would we have to reach to stop this negativity? How perfect would we have to be? When is there enough growth that we can move from self-judgment to self-acceptance?

Probably never.

But we can imagine the compassion a loving Creator would have for his favorite creation. And through choice, awareness and repetition, anything we can imagine, we can become.

Today I will choose to see myself with compassion. I will decide to take a point of view bigger than my judgment. I will imagine the adoration of an infinitely loving Creator for his favorite child. I will smile at a personal shortcoming, pick myself up, and once again try my best.

60

Comfort is Overrated

You will either step forward into growth
or you will step back into safety.

—Abraham Maslow
Motivation and Personality

The nature of life is evolution. With each moment, we own more of who we are, accepting ourselves as a center of consciousness. As we continue to meditate, we learn more and more to accept ourselves, warts, and all: our history, limitations, and shortcomings. We may even get comfortable with ourselves.

It's easy to think that comfort is the goal of spiritual and/or psychological work and believe that if we are uncomfortable, we must be doing something "wrong." But that's not the way it works.

We find comfort. This is true. And we become grounded in that feeling. And then life says something like, "Okay. Good. We have a foundation now. An experience of wholeness we can return to. Now it's time to expand, to take on more of life, more of consciousness; to take even more responsibility for the way life is playing out around us and for our brothers and sisters. It's time to own the deeper truth that we are expressions of Divine nature in this moment and in every moment."

And with this thought, we expand outward from the center. We own even more of consciousness than we thought was available to us. And it's uncomfortable. Like an arm that's been in a cast for six weeks—the cast comes off, and the skin hurts just from touching the air. Like this, we own this part of ourselves that's been unconscious and ignored, and it's uncomfortable.

But comfort is overrated. Own the discomfort. Embrace it. This is fantastic news. The discomfort means we're doing our jobs, that we're continuing to grow. Now we have the opportunity to find comfort even with this. Even with this new, more expanded experience of life and Self. We look out from our place in the center of it all, seeking our oneness with the world and asking from our Higher Self (or God, if you will) for help in seeing and taking the next step in the direction of our growth.

And as we step forward, we begin to find a new experience of comfort—the comfort of service to something greater than our ego and our small self needs. The comfort of consciousness on the move.

The universe is infinite. Consciousness, too, is unlimited. Our capacity to grow and own our place in consciousness is unbounded. If we want to be involved in this game of infinite growth and possibility, it will pay to make friends with our discomfort, for we're going to be seeing a lot of it.

Today I will own the temporary feeling of discomfort I may have without trying to get away from it or cover it up. I will feel the uncomfortable sensations in my body and then put my attention in the world rather than on the stories my mind tells me about the discomfort and what it means about me or the world. I will ask for guidance from something other than my ego about what the next right action might be. And I will take that next step, despite how uncomfortable I may feel.

The Real You

You are the consciousness which is the witness of all the drama, watching in amusement as the ego plays its games and dons different masks at different times. The real you is that ever-blissful, unchanging, blessed consciousness.

—Sri M

There is the real me. And there is the me I mistake myself to be, again and again. Whenever I tell myself I don't deserve to be happy or that you are somehow not worthy of my respect. Whenever I make choices from fear rather than from love. Whenever I choose to withdraw from life rather than step forward into the next moment. Whenever I let the pressure of these strange and trying times define me, rather than remember the me that I know myself as in my finest moments, that calls to me even in the darkest times, that I settle into each time I let the mantra guide me there.

Today I will remember with gratitude what a great gift I offer the world and myself, each time I step out of "ego games" and into the great reality of consciousness.

Trim Tabs

It's never too late to be what you might have been.

—George Eliot

The idea of change can feel overwhelming. Changing the way we think, how we feel about life, the habitual shape and flow of our moods, as well as our moodiness, can seem impossible. It may seem easier to give up, do nothing. Just have another cookie, watch another bad TV show or spend another hour on Instagram.

Change, though, isn't nearly as hard as we make it out to be. Massive, 180-degree change in our lives is not only possible, but can be relatively painless.

First, we meditate. Twice each day. Meditation breaks up the stresses that hold our habitual patterns so that each day it becomes easier to choose things that affirm life rather than keep us stuck, allowing us to build new habits and routines that lead to a better life.

And we don't have to change everything today. Just something. One small choice. We turn around the patterns of a lifetime by the smallest increments.

A helpful metaphor:

An ocean liner has a huge rudder that keeps it on course. But when the ship needs to turn, the rudder itself does not need to be muscled to the correct angle; instead, trim tabs on the trailing edge of the rudder do the work. These require minimal effort to move, but when they are adjusted, the pressure of the water against them pushes the rudder into position. With minute adjustments of the trim tabs, physics takes care of the rest, and the captain, navigator and helmsman are free to pay attention to the sea, the weather, possible hazards, constantly updating information to steer an ideal route to their eventual destination.

Like this, we can begin with the smallest changes in our behavior and know that it will become easier for us to move in the direction of well-being with each passing day. This is what nature intends and wants for us. And as we make these minute adjustments in the direction of our highest good, we will find nature rising to meet us and helping us to take the next step. And the next.

Today I will do one thing, no matter how small, that I think is in the direction God would have me move.

63

The Tracks of My Tears

When we teach Vedic Meditation, part of the course is learning about the stresses that have been stored in the cells of our body, building up in us since we began life in our mother's womb. Every time we have been overwhelmed by life or flooded by emotion, we have had some part of the experience locked in place within us. When something in our daily life echoes this experience from the past somehow, we are triggered into the full stress response of our prior experience, on top of whatever challenge exists in the situation in front of us.

It's like driving a car on a dirt road the day after a rain. If there was traffic there when it was wet, there are now ruts—sometimes deep and hard as cement. And if your tire falls into one, you're going to follow it until it ends. There is no turning out of it. This also happens inside us, when repeated triggering of negative thoughts and moods begin to wear grooves in the mind. We become entrenched in them, and it's increasingly difficult to break free.

Even if we can see ourselves overreacting and know that what's happening to us is out of proportion to our immediate situation, there are times we are completely powerless to do any thing about it. This is the bad news.

The good news? As we practice our meditation twice daily, these stored stresses literally melt away. The stuff of the mind within which they are stored becomes malleable, and what once was a rut has softened up so that we begin to have a choice. We start recognizing that what is happening within us is an old stress reaction, and we are able more and more to let it go and bring ourselves to present-moment awareness, responding to the circumstance of the moment, rather than being at the mercy of something that happened decades ago. We begin to find freedom.

What is required on my part is simply to meditate twice daily and remind myself each day that I am meant to enjoy life. No matter where I may find myself, there is a way for me to get from here to there. I can do it bit by bit, meditation by meditation, starting today.

Today I will do my twice-daily meditation, and during the day, when I find myself overreacting, I will pause, remind myself these are stresses leaving my body. And I will bring myself back to the present moment.

64

Don't You Want Somebody to Love?

That one I love who is incapable of ill will, and returns love for hatred. Living beyond the reach of 'I' and 'mine', and of pain and pleasure, full of mercy, contented, self-controlled, with all his heart and all his mind given to Me—with such a one I am in love.

—*Bhagavad Gita*
Chapter XII, verses 13-14

We often speak about finding happiness. But is that our job in life, our only purpose? No. Happiness is simply a side effect of finding our purpose. Happiness is an indication we are on the right track. It's a barometer within, giving us a moment-by-moment idea of how we're doing.

Our purpose, though, has to do with others—these humans we find ourselves having to understand, live with, find compassion for, tolerate. Our purpose has to do with our interactions with them. It has to do with learning to allow ourselves to love and be loved, finding unity here in all this diversity.

And the question arises: How do we love when others don't behave the way we'd like them to? How can we love people whose imperfections are so glaring, who come up short in their ability to love us?

And the answer is: *How can we not?*

We are built for love. Our emotional/hormonal system is designed for love. Our sense of well-being is dependent upon love. Love is an action. Love is a choice. Love is a flow. This flow of love is the healing power of the universe, of nature itself.

In our limited understanding of love, we see two paths. The first is to find someone who can love us; the second is to find someone we can love, wholly and without reservation.

When we feel empty, alone and needy, it makes sense that we would seek to be loved by someone else, for, after all, we have nothing to give. We are empty. We need to be filled up. And yet, we never are.

No one in the history of the world has been able to fill the emptiness of another in any sustainable fashion. Maybe for a time. A day, a week, a month, a year. But it will always cease to work, and we will be left needy once again.

As twice-daily meditators, we begin to find ourselves happy for no apparent reason. We learn to stop trying to find fulfillment "out there," and begin to recognize that it is only available within. We begin to find the idea of loving another, giving to another, actually plausible. We begin to realize we have something to offer the world, and we recognize that the times we feel most right are when we are being of service, giving of ourselves. So, we find someone to love. Romantically, maternally, fraternally. And what if this other doesn't want our love?

This is the beauty of the system. If I need love from you, I am at your mercy. You may choose to give or withhold love, and I then have to beg, plead, coerce, shame, force, manipulate or bargain with you to get the love I need. I have no control. If I want *to love*, all the control is in my hands.

I can love you whether you want me to or not. I can love you whether you know I'm doing it or not. I can love you even if you act as if you don't know I'm alive. I can love you in spite of your difficulties with me. I can love you despite your resistance. I can love you *because of* your resistance. In a word, I can love you for being exactly who you are. I can love you anytime, anywhere.

I do not need your permission to love you. And I do not require you to love me. Everything I need is provided by Self, the inner state. I am filled, daily, with Self, and I give of this fullness because it is my nature. Because it is what I am here to do. Love.

And sometimes, I love by letting you love me.

Love is why I am here.

Today I will insist on sending love to someone who, in my most judgmental of thoughts, doesn't deserve it. I will find one redeeming quality in someone I find difficult to love. I will let someone close to me off the hook for their crimes, real or imagined. I will let myself off the hook for my own crimes, real or imagined. I will invite God into the equation to show me how to do these seemingly impossible things, and I will let HerHimThemIt do that through me.

65

The Secret

I love to think of nature as an unlimited broadcasting station,
through which God speaks to us every hour, if we will only tune in.

—George Washington Carver

I believe that there is a subtle magnetism in Nature, which, if we
unconsciously yield to it, will direct us aright.

—Henry David Thoreau

All day, every day, we are receiving information from nature that we experience as a knowingness within. When we choose present moment awareness rather than our speculating mind, direct communication with the laws of nature is the payoff.

We are all individual expressions of nature itself. Nature wants nothing of us but to evolve. All we need to do is pay attention and allow ourselves to be led in the direction of evolution.

And as we pay attention in this simple way, we discover a great thing: Nature does not speak in code. It wants us to know. As we make ourselves available to it, nature is letting us in on the secret. And the secret is, *there are no secrets.*

There is no hidden passageway, no special handshake, no secret elixir. There is in each moment, always, one step to take that is more in the direction of evolution than any other step. Paying attention to the flow of nature allows us to see that one most evolutionary next step.

In each moment, we have the choice of falling into speculation and trying to "figure things out"—stay safe, get what we need, keep from losing what we have—or being in present moment awareness. Being here. Feeling our oneness with nature and taking in the information that oneness would have us know.

Today I will stay out of speculation. I will remain present to the voice of nature. When I fall into speculation, I will simply choose to be present. Again. And again.

66

Ego Was the Helper;
Ego Is the Bar

*You work and worry and then, just as you're getting comfortable
pulling focus, they move you to operator. And same thing there.
When you finally feel like you know what you're doing, they make
you a DP (director of photography). No wonder I sweat so much.*

—Tony, DP

Ego was the helper; ego is the bar.

—Sri Aurobindo
The Supramental Manifestation

The ego is how we come to know ourselves. The "terrible twos" is that time in development when I begin to recognize that I am separate from the world, that wanting my mother to do something does not make it happen. Thus begins my movement toward individuation, self-reliance, self-identity. I learn how to distinguish myself from others, from the crowd. How to stand out. How to excel, or if not, then how to not even get involved in these games other humans are playing. I discover where and how I fit, as well as my gifts and shortcomings. I begin to understand who is my tribe, my people, and who most fully reflects me to myself.

And just when I think I'm getting this figured out, I discover that to continue to evolve, I must step beyond each of these differentiating qualities to the place where I am at-one-with everyone and everything. I must begin to transcend all these ideas of difference to know myself as the oneness, as nature, as life itself.

Life is made up of these two selves: our small self individuality, and our large Self universality. Our journey in life is first to know the one absolutely so that we may transcend it and be the other. I know myself as "me," individuality, so that I may then begin to understand myself as "I," universality.

And then? And then I transcend even this duality and know myself as both, together. Individual and universal, at the same time.

Why? Because that's the way it works. This movement, this learning, is the way of life. Because the movement from knowing nothing, to individuation, to oneness, to All-ness, is the evolution toward an ever greater, more expanded, enjoyable, and productive experience of myself here in the world.

Today I will realize that no matter how loud the voice of the ego may be, there is something I am that is more. There is something I am that is beyond it. There is something I am growing toward, and if I simply choose to stop listening to the constant voice of the ego, in the silence behind that voice, I will begin to hear this something and recognize it as what I am.

67

Richard the Poet

Wherever a man turns, he can find someone who needs him.

—Albert Schweitzer

Many years ago, I had a friend known as Richard the Poet. "Friend" is perhaps not the right word because I'm not sure Richard had friends. He was someone who did not suffer fools. Richard was bipolar, brilliant and unmedicated, and he had seen God in some fashion. He was the perfect example of the truth of Western culture that those we might see as "other" would, at other times and in other places, be seen as saints.

Richard let me talk to him because he could see that I, too, was serious about this God business. I needed to know something that he knew, so I asked his advice and counsel. Richard suggested that if I wanted to get in touch with God, I could write to him. So, each morning for a while, I would park myself at the kitchen table with a pot of strong coffee, a pack of Marlboros, a pen, and a spiral-bound notebook.

At the top of a page, I would write this prayer: God, please help me to write that which will be pleasing to you, and which will bring me closer to you. Thank you, God. Amen.

I would draw a line under this prayer, and then I would write. Sometimes just free form, sometimes questions and answers—the questions from "me," the answers, seemingly, from God, the pen moving almost of its own accord. It was brilliant. There was a voice inside me that had been waiting to speak, and it spoke. Beautifully. Positively. Like I imagine the book *Conversations with God* to be (though I haven't read it). I would write, and then once a week or so, I would report to Richard, and we would discuss. The writing and the conversations with Richard gave me much comfort.

One day I wrote a question, and the answer came back, "I don't know." I was stunned. I sat there, pen poised, for the longest time.

Then I wrote, "What do you mean, 'You don't know?' You're God. You're supposed to know everything."

The answer came back, "I never said I was God."

This stopped me for a moment. I realized that, indeed, the voice had never made this claim. It was an assumption on my part. So, I wrote, "Well, is God in there?"

The answer came back, "Of course."

I watched in that moment as a mental structure that had constrained me and my ideas of the Divine broke apart and dissolved. I was left with a feeling of spaciousness and expansiveness that was breathtaking. I was no longer stuck with a finite idea of this infinite thing that God must be. I had been given a new level of freedom.

I was reminded of Richard recently and felt such gratitude. When he was able to fight through his insanity, his generosity of spirit was astounding. He was another soul struggling through the confusion of life toward some light he had seen in the distance, willing to reach back to lend a hand to a fellow traveler. I hope that in my best moments I live up to his example.

Today I will remind myself that, regardless of how much difficulty I seem to be having, someone else might be having a harder time than me. I will keep my eyes open, and when I find that person, I will be sure to lend a hand.

68

Existence, Consciousness, Bliss

Sat-Chit-Ananda/Saccidananda:

Existence and Thought and Joy.
Of the One self-existing or universal Spirit.
Brahman. Totality.

—Sir M. Monier-Williams
A Sanskrit-English Dictionary

at = Existence, Is-ness, Truth. That which is, has always been, will always be. That which is behind all thoughts, feelings, concepts, structure is this—pure Being.

Chit = Consciousness, Awareness. Life that is aware of itself. The Veda describes the birth of awareness from the oneness of existence as the desire of life to know itself. The desire of life to be able to see itself, experience itself and forget itself in part so that it could look back upon itself and feel the joy of recognition. Oh, yes! This is me! This is what we are. The great I Am. Life itself.

Ananda = Transcendental Bliss. The experience that everything is okay, exactly as it is; that I am okay, exactly as I am. Happiness that simply is, dependent on nothing, at the effect of nothing. It is the very nature of life itself, our least excited state, behind the layers of thought, feeling and ideation, beyond the sensations of the physical body and emotions. Bliss is the nature of what we are. Simply by being, we are the embodiment of happiness.

This is the truth of our nature. We are, we know that we are, and what we are is the experience of bliss.

In practical terms, this means simply that we are meant to enjoy life. It is our birthright. It is our assignment.

How do we fulfill this assignment? Well, that is the work of a lifetime. To begin, however, we take this as a given: I am meant to enjoy my life. And if in this moment I am not able to find this enjoyment, knowing that bliss is available opens me at least to the possibility of it.

Saccidananda. Existence, Consciousness, Bliss is and always has been your true nature. See if you can find an experience of it today.

Today I will remember that I am meant to enjoy my life. I will open to the possibility that no matter what the facts of my life are in this moment, there is a way for me to find an experience of "okay-ness" here and now with things exactly as they are. I will ask not what needs to be changed out there to experience this happiness, but rather what can be changed within. And I will open myself to being guided by the movement of life itself in finding this experience of bliss.

69

The Golden Age

*I swear I think now that every thing without
exception has an eternal soul!
The trees have, rooted in the ground!
The weeds of the sea have!
The animals!
I swear I think there is nothing but immortality!
That the exquisite scheme is for it,
and the nebulous float is for it, and the cohering is for it!
And all preparation is for it—and identity is for it—and life
and death are altogether for it!*

—Walt Whitman
"Leaves of Grass"

The Veda tells the story of an ancient time when consciousness was full, and all were born enlightened. For eons, people had worked toward this Golden Age through meditation, study, correction of the intellect and an insistence on finding the "something more" that each knew was here. And with that insistence came success: self-awareness, self-knowledge, discovering the truth within.

As more people discovered this truth and knew it to be within each other, consciousness expanded. The more people knew the oneness within, the more they could see it all around them and pass it on.

Consciousness, the one thing, was seen clearly by person after person and was purified by this seeing. The oneness became more wholly one (of course not really, but it seemed so), and when 1% of the people were enlightened—it began to spread like wildfire. Suddenly it was one person in every ten who knew the oneness within themselves, and then, like water flowing into a long-dry lakebed, no place could remain dry for long. The people wondered at their long resistance and insistence on making life hard for themselves and others when the truth was so simple.

Thus, a Golden Age was born, when enlightenment was one's birthright and struggle a thing of the past. Bliss, happiness, and unity were the order of the day. Suffering ceased. Babies were born enlightened, knowing the truth of life. Generations thrived with the sun of consciousness bright and undeniable within them. The tools of meditation and study were put away.

Then one day, a child was born with the light obscured. It was hidden behind false darkness and wrong ideas. It was as it had been long ago, but no one knew how to help anymore. Slowly, then not so slowly, the Golden Age became a dark age again, and humans had to make sense of suffering and peace with death and despair. All felt lost.

Until someone, finally, insisted that there had to be more.

They demanded from nature to be shown the way to truth once again. Nature responded to this demand from itself, and the practice of meditation and study once again was found. Little pockets and pools of light began to shine in the vast darkness of the planet, lending hope, at last, to those with the eyes and the need to see.

This is now where we find ourselves.

Today I will practice my meditation, knowing it is my responsibility to shine my light into the darkness, and I will insist on seeing that light within others.

70

Sometimes Life Hurts

It is difficult to find happiness in oneself,
but it is impossible to find it anywhere else.

—Arthur Schopenhauer

Being a meditator and living a "spiritual" life doesn't give us freedom from pain. It's not about making a mood of "everything's fine."

Sometimes life hurts.

People die, relationships change and disappear. Hearts are broken. Meditating doesn't mean we can avoid these pains. In fact, because we try as much as possible to be present to life, the pain itself might be even more poignant for a meditator. But what the meditator has is:

1. The capacity not to turn pain into suffering by asking "why me?" or "why him?" or "what does it all mean?" Being a meditator means we don't need to fall into the endless speculation that leads only to suffering. The pain arrives, the pain moves through, the pain moves on. Next...

2. The certain knowledge that all change is progressive change, that regardless of how deeply something may hurt now, it's happening for a reason. All things happen for all reasons. If something is falling apart, it is doing so to make room for the

next something—we have no space for a new wardrobe until we clean out our closet. Nature is no different. Room must be made for the new, and the next something by definition will be an evolution of the current something. This is all nature knows how to do: evolve. This is all we, as nature, will do: evolve. And finally;

3. The knowledge that happiness is a choice that is available within, in this moment, and nothing outside ourselves can add to nor take away from the happiness that we are. When we feel sorrow, it is an indication, and perhaps a challenge, for us to find a definition of happiness that is wide enough to include even this—whatever "this" happens to be.

Today I will allow myself to feel my feelings fully, without letting them determine my state of being. I am a happy, joyous, and free expression of nature, regardless of this ache, pain or sorrow that tells me I shouldn't be.

71

Sadhana

We do not distinguish between life and sadhana ...
In our yoga, there must be a continuous life activity,
serving as a channel of sacrifice,
self-consecration to God; things like meditation and prayer have
their own timings. The sadhana goes on all the time.
Sadhana does not consist only in meditation or asanas (postures).
Sadhana is in the culturing of one's consciousness, right from head to
toe Godward, utilising each occasion to let the consciousness growing
towards God express itself in our day-to-day movements,
transforming the entire life into a rhythm of God.

—M.P. Pandit
Under the Mother's Banner

Twice daily, we pause for 20 minutes and meditate, connecting more deeply with our innermost self. Then, we have the rest of our day. How can we use these hours to help grow ourselves? Our tradition suggests that our experiences can be used to help us see ourselves as God sees us—as pure, full, and perfect expressions of nature itself.

The Sanskrit term sadhana, which is translated by B.K.S. Iyengar in the *Yoga Sutras of Patanjali* as "a discipline undertaken in the pursuit of a goal," generally refers to any practice used to move toward the goal of union with the Divine. Our meditation would be seen as one form of sadhana, as would certain types of yoga, breathing exercises (pranayama), singing, chanting, or praying. Selfless service for a teacher or working in a yoga studio, ashram or soup kitchen may all be seen as forms of sadhana.

The great Vedic teacher and master Sri Aurobindo said that "All life is yoga," meaning that all aspects of one's life, not just these specific practices, can be used to achieve union, yoga, with the Divine. The Mother, Sri Aurobindo's partner in teaching, in answer to a question about this same subject, states further:

"All that we do, anything we do, may be used to bring us closer to God. All it takes from me is to set this as my intention and to remember, whenever it occurs to me, that I am doing this thing, whatever it may be, as an act of love."

Today I will remember at least once at the beginning of the day and again at the end of the day to dedicate all of myself and my actions toward the goal of wholeness. I will set an intention to be of loving service in everything I do.

72

The Mind Never Seems to Stop

Feelings are not "states." I'm not a "sad person," though I may have sadness. I'm not an angry person, though I may experience myself that way. These feelings—our emotional response to a given experience—are rather short-lived, lasting something like a minute and a half. But then our thoughts get involved and the feeling is enlivened again and again, our mind propelling it like a beachball kept aloft by the crowd in a stadium.

The mind never seems to stop. It's a running commentary of how I'm doing, how you think I'm doing, how you're not doing it the way I want you to do it and what that means about us. It's "if you loved me, you wouldn't _____. If you really loved me, you'd _____."

The mind is not broken. It's not out to get me. I'm simply using it in a way it's not designed to be used.

The mind, our intellect, is brilliant at a few things.

First, it's an incredible historian. It can tell me what happened and why it happened. It can see the patterns, turns and players. The mind is great at this. But then I misuse it by trying to structure my future based upon what it's telling me about my past. I hold on and try to steer things into alignment by thinking them so. This never works.

Second, the intellect is great at solving problems. When I drive from the Valley to Mid-Wilshire, the intellect will add the time of day to the equation and then tell me what route to take. And all along the way, it will measure my progress, adjusting as I move forward to find the least traffic, the most open, direct path from here to there until finally, I am where I want to be. Success! When I figure out my schedule for the week, put something together from Ikea, work out the scene that takes us from Act I to Act II in my screenplay—these are problems the intellect is designed to solve.

I misuse it when I see my lack of happiness as a problem to be solved. Then my mind will tell me all the reasons I'm unhappy: you're too old, too fat, no one loves you, no one cares, happiness isn't available, the world is a bad place. Most of these things I can't control. And how do I feel then, after my mind has told me all this? Still unhappy and now hopeless to boot.

The mind can't help itself. It becomes aware of sensations moving through the body and explains what they mean. This sensation is sadness, and here's the story of why I'm sad. It will take the thought "dog," then move to "old Rover," then how old Rover died and how lonely I've been since then, he was the last true friend I ever had ...

I can't stop it. The mind is going to do pretty much what it wants most of the time. But I can step away from it and have a point of view on it rather than be identified with it.

When we meditate, we transcend the mind and experience what we are beyond thoughts and feelings. So, when we find ourselves overwhelmed with these thoughts and feelings in our day, we can remind ourselves that this is simply what the mind does, and we can become present to the sensations passing through the body.

We can get present to the five senses and let the mind do what it does. We don't have to listen to it. And the more we practice being in the world rather than in our thoughts about the world, the less power the mind will have over how we experience anything.

And as we continue to meditate twice a day, over time the mind begins to quiet down on its own, and we begin to find here with the eyes open the same peace we find in meditation.

Today I will remind myself to get present to the world, rather than to my thoughts about the world. I will remind myself to listen to my friend rather than my thoughts about what she's saying. I will remind myself that my life is not a problem to be solved but rather an experience to be had, and I will make myself available to that experience.

73

Trombone Playing

Forever alive, forever forward,
Stately, solemn, sad, withdrawn,
baffled, mad, turbulent, feeble, dissatisfied,
Desperate, proud, fond, sick, accepted by men, rejected by men,
They go! they go! I know that they go, but I know not where they go,
But I know that they go toward the best—toward something great.

—Walt Whitman
"Song of the Open Road, 13"

Who am I? A case could be made that this is the only question worth asking and perhaps the only question we are ever asking.

As I write this, I am listening to classical trombone music.

Once upon a time, many years ago, I was a trombone player. I worked and worked and worked to be good at it, and for one brief moment, I was. Driving to Los Angeles from Montana, taking the long way through Oregon and down the coast, my friend and I stopped on a beach outside of Eureka in Northern California near sunset.

This being the '70s and us being hippies, we threw off our clothes and swam naked through the surf. Afterward, I took out my trombone and played every Charlie Parker song I knew, still naked and with the sun setting before me.

On that beach in those moments, I was brilliant. I was a trombone player. Shortly after that, my trombone career was curtailed by a profound lack of self-worth and self-esteem.

I moved on to being a bass player—never very good. A handyman. A taxi driver. A bartender. An actor. A meditation teacher.

And before that moment in the sun on the beach with my trombone, I had been a farmer, a factory worker, a carney, a bum.

I have also been (and remain) a brother, an uncle, a student, a son, a father, a lover, a husband, and on and on. The list of the things all of us have been—from newborn baby to reader of this essay is almost endless. Many things we once were, we are no longer. Many things we are we will cease being, including "alive in a body."

And yet there is some part of me that remembers these things, at least many of them. There is that in me that remembers being 4 years old, that remembers the smell of trombone slide cream, that remembers meeting Frank Rosolino, a brilliant trombonist at Dante's Jazz Club in North Hollywood, that remembers waking this morning and beginning this day. That awareness, that "I Am," is, was and always will be. What is that? How do I know that? How may I know myself as that?

This is the work of our days and nights. This is what we are here to discover. For by discovering this, we uncover not only the secret of our own lives but the secret of life itself. For that, "I Am" within is the same as Totality Itself. It is the Self that underlies all things. It is the source of happiness and fulfillment, of all creativity, all capacity for love. It is everything I have ever wanted and everything I ever have wanted to be. And it is right here, within me, in my least excited state.

All I need to do is continue to meditate, dropping into that least excited state twice each day. And then reminding myself, whenever I can remember to, that whatever it seems I am in any moment, other than Self, is temporary. And asking, "where is this other thing I must be that doesn't change?"

Today I will take pains to see past the relative in myself and the people around me so that I may begin to recognize the truth of life, the truth of I Am.

Note: This "Thought" was written for an old friend, John Wickham, who continues to play trombone, and who was always one of my heroes of the horn. He was brilliant 50 years ago, and I'm sure he's only gotten better.

74

Sadhana Part II, or Living in the Material World

Sadhana, spiritual exertion towards an intended goal.

—Wikipedia, the free encyclopedia

S ome teachers and systems tell us that to live a "spiritual life," we must give up the things of this world—that these things are not important, that there is only one thing worth having, one thing worth knowing: the truth of your higher oneness with God. But we may ask: "What about rent? What about my career, my love life, my bank account, the new lens for my camera? What about all these things of the relative world? Am I supposed to pretend these things don't matter to me?"

Vedic meditation is known as "the householder's technique." It is not for those who want to leave society, go off to the caves in the jungle above Rishikesh, India, and spend the next two months or ten years in meditation. Our practice is for those of us who have families, jobs, careers; who are of the world and wish to remain so and want to know the truth of spirit within.

There is more we can do than just meditate twice a day. There is a way to bring more consciousness to our experience of life, even as we are in the world. We practice *sadhana*—offering all that we do to the Divine or to the universal spirit or the flow of nature—whichever concept works for you. This is the yoga of works. It's karma yoga: Seeking unity (yoga) through action done (karma). It is described by the great sage Sri Aurobindo in *Letters on Yoga* this way:

> *"The ordinary life consists of work for personal aim and satisfaction of desire... The [Bhagavad] Gita's yoga consists of the offering of one's work as a sacrifice to the Divine, the conquest of desire, egoless and desireless action, [love] for the Divine... the sense of unity with all creatures, oneness with the Divine."*

This can seem like a tall order. Some of us work in snake pits of ego that may feel like battlegrounds. Some of us do work that requires all our attention, perhaps intensely so. How are we to dedicate our work to the Divine? Again, from Sri Aurobindo:

"If you can't yet remember the Divine all the time you are working, it does not greatly matter. To remember and dedicate at the beginning and give thanks at the end ought to be enough for the present."

And if the idea of the Divine is not appealing, then simply remembering "the sense of unity with all creatures" will suffice to help raise my awareness out of the morass that the relative world can become. And then there is this to remember: if I am dedicating my work to something greater than my individuality, that something is waiting to respond in kind to flow through me as this giving. Again, as Sri Aurobindo so eloquently states:

"*[This] is a great secret of sadhana, to know how to get things done by the Power behind or above instead of doing all by the mind's effort... Strength is all right for the strong—but aspiration and the*

Grace answering to it are not altogether myths; they are great realities of the spiritual life."

Today I will dedicate all the work I do as service to something greater than myself—to the Divine, to the world, to my fellow man, to my family, to my co-workers, to my idea of what is right.

75

Negative Self-Talk

We are spirit, having a human experience. We walk around in these animal suits, always concerned with survival. Anything in our experience that might be seen as threatening can trigger our fight/flight/freeze/fawn response. Then the amygdala goes into overdrive, and our more-modern brain parts begin to spin stories from the past related to these triggers. We think: *How did we respond before, and what do we need to do now to assure our safety? What should we have done to avoid ending up here?*

These thoughts then trigger more survival responses in our body, which leads to more thoughts. It goes around and around, and we end up with a steady stream of scary ideas running through our heads with the feeling of impending doom and anxiety looming over us.

Negative self-talk is one of the most debilitating experiences we can have. The voices might begin the moment our eyes open in the morning and continue through the day, fading only during an extreme workout, a yoga class, a great movie or lovemaking. Some of us will use a drink or a joint to dull the voices; some an obsession or fantasy—someone we're attracted to, a new car, a better job, winning the lottery, even getting revenge against someone who has "wronged" us.

These thoughts can be so all-pervasive that we almost cease noticing them or seeing them as something we can change. Our minds may tell us we deserve to have these thoughts because we are bad or worthless. It will tell us we are separate, different and worse than the rest of humanity, and this thought will amp up the negative ruminations to an even higher degree.

But we can arrest the process, much as we might step in if we saw two kids on a playground fighting over a toy. Just by interrupting the proceedings, we allow for the possibility of change.

No one deserves to be spoken to the way our mind sometimes speaks to us. Ever. Nor is anything ever served by this kind of talk.

If you've ever been berated by an authority figure, be it a parent, teacher, principal or cop, you know that it rarely leads to change. Shame, yes. But almost never change. Because voices like this don't tell us we have done something wrong; they tell us we *are* something wrong. And if we are something wrong, then we probably aren't capable of change anyway.

What allows change to occur is love. It's an act of self-love to stop long enough to notice the voices and what they're saying. Becoming aware of the barrage of negativity we subject ourselves to brings it into the light of day. And once it has been seen, we can begin to change it.

There's a saying in recovery groups that "I take care of the thought, and let God take care of the obsession." This takes into account that this negative, critical thinking has become a habit. If we've been at it for a few decades, it's worn a groove in our minds, and it's going to keep occurring in us, at least for the time being. But it can change.

We begin the change by noticing. We check in with our thoughts and hear the negative words, the self-disgust and self-hatred. We say, *"Oh. That voice again. Saying the same thing it always says. Would God speak to me this way? No. So this must not be the voice of God. Thanks for sharing."*

And then we turn away from it without trying to change it. By doing so, we turn it over to God. Or, if you'd rather, to nature, a Higher Power or your Higher Self. We turn it over, letting this greater force deal with it.

And then, we get present. We come to our senses. We notice the quality of light wherever we find ourselves. We listen to the murmur of the wind in the trees, the rush of traffic, the hiss of the espresso machine at Starbucks. We feel our feet on the ground, the breeze against our cheek. We taste the mint we just had, smell the scent of winter in the air. We get present to what is, rather than to the thoughts about why we don't deserve any of it.

It's extremely difficult to remember to do, but terribly simple once we begin. One time in the morning and once in the evening is a start. Eventually, we will find the way to do it throughout the day, gradually spending a bit less time with our inner critic and a bit more time with what is. And when "what is" takes up more space in our day than not, we will be pleasantly surprised at just how much life we find ourselves deserving of.

Today I will take care of the thought and let God take care of the obsession.

76

Love is the Currency
of the Universe

The teachings of Vedanta are very clear: There is only one thing. I Am. God Is. There is only one thing.

What is the I Am? What is God? If there is only one thing, the answer to both these questions must be the same.

How can this be? If there is only one thing, if my sense of being and the truth of God are the same, then why do I experience loneliness? How can I feel at times so unworthy, inept, and separate? If the truth of all is oneness, why is there so much hatred in the world, so much division, violence and judgment?

In one telling, the relative world—this experience we are having as separate and individual, you over there, me over here—exists for the sole purpose that this one thing might have the joy of loving itself in all its disparate expressions. This means all colors, shapes, sizes, ages, ethnicities, genders, sexual preferences, sexual identities, income brackets, opinions, politics, any and all formulations possible. This is the "what." This is the "why." This is what the one thing wants, always.

So, why should I care? Why should I go out of my way to love when hurt, anger and frustration might be all that I feel? When "God" feels as far away as possible. When there's not an ounce in me that feels safe enough to reach out or offer anything to anyone, ever. Because to love when everything in you says "no," is the point of it all. Loving someone who looks like me, sounds like me, smells like me, aches like me is the easy bit. Loving someone who feels wholly "other,"—*that* builds a muscle. That is the work of a spiritual warrior. And if it were easy, it wouldn't be worth doing.

When I insist on loving despite every feeling and thought that says "no," I am doing the work of identifying with the highest expression of Self that is possible in this human form. I am saying that despite all these impulses in me to stay small, separate and "against," I am choosing to know myself as an expression of nature in its most subtle and beautiful form, as an expression of God Itself.

Love is the currency of the universe. Let me find my place to spend some today.

77

We are Made of Star-Stuff

Once upon a time, billions of years ago, the matter from the Big Bang became the stars. Around some of the stars, planets formed. Upon some of these planets, life arose. That life is what we are, made of the same stuff as the stars.

The Upanishads are one of the main sources of Vedic wisdom. "Upanishad" means something like "sitting down at the feet (or source) of the knowledge." This implies the need to empty ourselves of what we think we know so that something of the Truth may be poured into us.

The writings speak of the makeup of the universe, the underlying field of all that Is, and the building blocks of all that Is, which is *Brahman*. Totality.

They say this field is consciousness, pure Being, and that it may be experienced by anyone willing to look for it. The Brihadaranyaka Upanishad begins with a peace chant that states the whole Truth in one verse.

In Sanskrit, it is:

Om. Purnamadah purnamidam purnatpurnamudachyate;
Purnasya purnamadaya purnamevavashishyate
Om shantih shantihi—

The English translation is:
Om (the sound of Creation),
That is infinite, and this (universe) is infinite.

The infinite proceeds from the infinite.
After taking the infinite from the infinite,
Only the infinite remains.
Om, Peace peace

The infinite is all that is. God is all that is. Just as stardust pulled from our sun became this world, and man arose from this world, we too are made of stardust. From the infinite Brahman proceeds this endless universe, and all that is in this universe, too, cannot be anything other than pervasive, eternal Brahman. We are made of God-stuff. There is nothing else we could be made of.

Today I will set aside my thoughts, feelings, and ideas of myself to find contact with this stuff of which I am made. I will remind myself that nothing, not even my resistance, can limit God; and I will ask of this infinite universe what it is that limitless God would have me do. And as one expression of God-stuff, I will recognize and insist upon my capacity to fulfill that assignment.

78

Pay Attention to What Is

The Vedic seers say that God is everywhere in every moment, every thing, always. What moves the Truth of God from potential to reality is our attention.

Modern science tells us everything in the universe is structured out of energy and information, including you and me. The power is of God, of the universe. It is the very stuff of which the universe is made—that which can neither be created nor destroyed. The energy simply IS.

We supply the information from our minds—the picture we each have of reality, most especially of ourselves in this reality. My experience then is a creation from this energy, shaped by my ideas. If I have ideas of myself as less-than, unhappy or unworthy—of life, love, and happiness—then this is the experience I will structure for myself.

The universe is waiting for a cue from me: *What kind of universe do you want me to be? What kind of experience do you want to have?* The thoughts of our today are the building blocks of our tomorrow.

We start wherever we can, from wherever we are. We don't jump from "I'm a worthless so-and-so" to "I'm the king of the world." We look around and find one thing to be grateful for. Like breathing. Like the ability to smile. Like having the eyes to read this writing, the computer or paper to read it on, the time to sit and take a moment to improve the quality of your life, the mind to comprehend what you've read, the freedom to hit "Delete" or "Forward," the freedom to laugh or to cry, the freedom to choose to embrace the day or to wait for the doom that's sure to come if our speculating mind has its way.

Today I will choose to pay attention to what is right in my world, letting what is "wrong" in my world or other people take care of itself.

79

A Decent Regret

I once was told by a psychiatrist, one of the wisest men I've ever met, that guilt is by and large a worthless emotion. His theory is that the feeling is a leftover from our evolutionary past, a built-in biochemical consequence to any action that takes us out of the flow of the herd; for when a herd animal wanders away alone, he attracts predators, thereby endangering the whole. Guilt is one of nature's ways of assuring our continued survival.

The literal definition of "sin" is "to miss the mark." To treat my mistakes as anything more than this is egotism. Bill Wilson, the co-founder of Alcoholics Anonymous, suggested the notion of "a decent regret" as appropriate in most circumstances where we have come up short.

In truth, anything in my past can be judged negatively by me in the present. The person I am today has grown through the experience of yesterday. I have learned from my "mistakes." I have evolved. By definition, I will be more conscious today than I was yesterday, and I will be able to see how I might have done things differently, how I might do things today. This means if I am inclined to feel guilty, I will always be able to find something to feel guilty about.

Though a sense of responsibility for our actions is essential in the survival of our social structure, guilt, as some of us experience it, can be far more detrimental than beneficial.

We humans learn by trial and error. This is our nature. Yet, so many of us feel guilty for "coming up short" in our lives. We treat ourselves as if we should know how to do things we've never done before, as if we're supposed to know how to choose a good romantic partner, how to stay in a long-term relationship, how to be a good parent, how to love; and yet all of these things, and so much more in our life, is on-the-job training. The mistakes and missteps are the process by which we grow, the way we find our path to a better life, to a better use of ourselves.

Stepping forward into the next unknown moment with the intention to show up as best we can, giving as much of ourselves as we can—this is what we can expect of ourselves. This is what we can ask of ourselves. And when we land ungracefully, when we miscalculate, we can have a "decent regret." We learn whatever lesson there is to learn and find the willingness to surrender the guilt, leaving ourselves open and available to try it—whatever it is—one more time.

Today I will make an effort to leave guilt and self-judgment aside. I will permit myself not to know how to do something, and I will do it anyway, as well as I can, trusting that I have been designed to learn in just this way.

80

Thousands of Candles

Thousands of candles can be lit from a single candle, and the life of the candle will not be shortened. Happiness never decreases by being shared.

—The Buddha (Siddhārtha Gautama)

What will I share with the world today, with the people in my world? What conditions must be met before I allow myself happiness? Do I need to lose more weight, make more money or find a new lover before I'll be happy?

Does my worrying improve anything? Does my presence enhance your life? When I enter a room today, am I bringing with me a cloud of anxiety or a breath of fresh air? If today's mood is the source of tomorrow's experience, how will I feel when my eyes open tomorrow morning?

These are just some of the questions we might ask ourselves on any given day. It is not enough simply to meditate morning and evening. Consciousness is primary—all else flows from it. We build our experience of the world first in our mind; then we live it out in our reality, again and again.

If we want a different world, we must build a different mind. To do this, we must pay attention to our thinking in a way that allows us to observe it rather than to be identified with it. We must ask ourselves, what kind of a world would I like this to be? What kind of me would I like to be? Then we look at our thinking to see if it is in the direction we would like to move. Happiness is always a good place to start.

Today I will insist on enjoying life.

81

Cosmic Consciousness

The first stage of enlightenment is referred to as "cosmic consciousness."
Meaning:
cos·mic - of or pertaining to the cosmos; immeasurably extended in time and space; vast.

Which leads us to:
cos·mos - the world or universe regarded as an orderly, harmonious system.

And then:
con·scious·ness - the state of being conscious; awareness of one's own existence, sensations, thoughts, surroundings, etc.
from *Dictionary.com Unabridged.*
Source location: Random House, Inc.

So what we end up with is:
Cosmic consciousness - "awareness of one's own existence" as "an orderly harmonious system," "immeasurably extended in time and space."
This is cosmic consciousness. Aware of ourselves as individuals; aware of ourselves as at-one-with the infinity of the universe.
This is not nearly as grandiose as it sounds. Really.

Modern physicists are often quoted as saying that the underlying truth of the universe can be described as the unified field. If this is true (and as a theory, it is one of the most successful of all time, though still as yet unproven), it means that there is only one thing, with each of us an individualized expression of this one thing. We are waves expressed from the unified field—each individual but also one part of the vast, infinite whole.

The Veda says much the same: there is only one thing, and each of us is an expression of that one thing. Further, that one thing is, in fact, consciousness itself.

- The universe is one thing.

- The one thing in the universe is consciousness.

- The universe is infinite.

- Therefore, consciousness is infinite.

- By definition, in an infinite field, every point is the center of the field.

- I exist. I know this because I am conscious.

- If I exist, and there is only one thing, then I must be that one thing.

- As a point in the infinite field of consciousness, I am the center of that infinite field. As are you, your mother, your father, your dentist and your third-grade teacher. As are we all.

- If we are all the center of this infinite field, we are all the same. We are all one.

Remembering this is our task at hand.

This is not about the grandiosity of the small self. It's about the grandeur of God. The majesty of God is what we are.

Today I will open my mind to the idea of infinity and my place at the center of it. I will look into the eyes of my fellows and imagine my oneness with each of them—especially those I seem to have a problem with.

Kumbh Mela

What amrita is to gods... so to humans is Ganga water.

—*Mahabharata*
XIII.26.49

Kumbh Mela is a fair held every three years at one of the holy places of India, and every 12 years, there is the Maha (great) Kumbh Mela, where over the course of six weeks, some 110 to 130 million people gather.

Kumbha means "water pot." In the context of Kumbh Mela, it refers to the pot-holding amrita, the nectar of immortality. There is a very long, though entertaining, story about how this amrita was churned from the sea in ancient times by the gods and the demons.

It involves a mountain as a churning stick, a serpent as a rope and a task so vast the gods could not do it alone, so they convinced the demons to help them. Many fine things were churned from the sea—the first physician, the chariot of the sun, Lakshmi, the goddess of wealth—but the last and best prize was the amrita. The gods and demons battled for a thousand years over who would keep this sacred nectar. And when the gods finally won the tug of war, as they were carrying the pot off to heaven, four drops fell to earth. These spots are said to be the holiest of holy, and these are the four points where the fairs occur.

Allahabad, at the confluence of the Yamuna, Ganga and Saraswati Rivers, is one of the places that host the great fair, where those millions of people gather solely to find connection—with their brothers and sisters, God, spirit, and the Higher Self.

What does this mean for Westerners?

In practical terms, it means that one may attend this festival, sleep in freezing cold tents with few or no blankets, not have one moment of silence through the day or night, with loudspeakers blaring bhajans and lectures and crowds of people crying out.

You may walk for countless kilometers in crowds large enough to be seen by satellite and never encounter a cross word, never feel frightened or crowded, be welcomed by the Indians with smiles and open arms, have a tangible experience of unity with these fellow humans from the time you arrive to the time you leave and beyond. You may be filled with bliss for no apparent reason, just simply because. And then, you'll wonder why you only planned for five days here, when obviously you should have come for the whole six weeks. And you'll know that in 12 years, you'll be able to find a much better tent.

The only thing anybody ever really wants is to feel connected, to feel love. If one travels halfway around the world for a festival that is dedicated to that connectedness, achieving it is as simple as stepping out onto the road and smiling at each person you meet. But of course, we don't really need to go to all that trouble.

We can choose to feel this connection at any time, simply by ceasing to insist on the ways we keep ourselves separate from each other. And feeling the connectedness that is always there, that is truly what we are —not as an idea, an ideal or a *maybe someday it might be nice to feel that*—but right now, in this next moment. For beyond the ego, the body and the ideas of difference that keep us separate, apart from and miserable, there is only oneness. And this oneness is what we are.

Bolo Ganga mai ki jai!

Sing praises to Ma Ganga!
Victory to Mother Ganga!

Today I will recognize that those around me who may seem troubled are really only looking for connection, and I will offer it to them, at least by knowing for myself that we all are one.

Come to Your Senses

Mindfulness is the term used to describe our awareness of what is, rather than our speculation *about* what is and how it should be different.

Each day, in each moment, we have the option to be in the state of speculation—thinking about the past, worrying about the future—or in present-moment awareness. As we continue on this path of meditation and study, we find that speculation always leads only to suffering. Nothing ever gets "figured out," no matter how long or often we think about it. And by going into speculation, we take ourselves out of the very place—this present moment—from where we gather the information we need to make the choices of our lives.

In other words, speculation takes us out of life. And it is this being out of our life that causes us to suffer.

The good news? To step out of this suffering requires only that we choose, with each moment, to be here. To be present to our five senses. To be present to each other. To be present to the world. It's as simple as choosing to do so.

Today I will choose, at least once in the morning and once in the evening, to be absolutely present to my senses, to be absolutely alive in the world.

A Full Cup

I think I'm beginning to learn something about it.

The final words spoken by Pierre-Auguste Renoir as he put away his brushes, having painted all day from his bed.
Source: *Renoir, My Father* by Jean Renoir

There is a story about a university professor who visits a Zen master, ostensibly to learn from him. As the master prepares tea for his guest, the professor talks on and on about Zen. When the tea is ready, the master begins to pour a cup for the professor. He fills the cup and continues to pour, the tea overflowing and spilling out onto the table.

The professor says, "Stop, sir! The cup is full!"

The master replies, "You are like this cup. How can I teach you when you are already so full?"

When we're young, we're continually called upon to perform in situations where we have no experience. By definition, nearly everything we do is new. We've never been in fifth grade before. Never sung in the church choir before. Never kissed a boy, a girl, never ridden a bike or driven a car. Taking the SATs, drinking a beer, studying for college finals, applying for a job, getting married—there's a first time for everything.

Depending on our personality, our parents and our emotional and mental makeup, we develop our own recipe of asking questions, studying, trusting our instincts and/or faking it—pretending we know things we can't possibly know and deathly afraid someone will discover our deceit.

As we grow, of course, we gain experience. We survive these things, and we learn legitimate tools. Each of us has our strengths, and ideally, we find a way to put these strengths to work for us. But there are those pockets of life where we may still be pretending we know what we're doing. We've pretended something forever and so, we have never allowed ourselves to learn.

Sometimes we've faked something so well that we no longer even know we are faking it. It's gone underground, and we just continue to behave as if we know what we're doing. If someone pokes us there, we become defensive. How can we let go of this? How can we empty our cup and become teachable again?

We embrace the idea of humility. We let go of thinking we know what we're doing or acting like we know what we're doing. We let go of the idea we've done this before, for truly, every day is new, every moment is unique.

This is always the case. But sometimes, we forget. We go on automatic. We check out and fall into speculation. Thinking, instead of being. We leave the world behind and tell ourselves we are waiting for something interesting to happen, and when it does, we'll come back out to play. This is the arrogance of the full cup.

When I can walk into a situation fresh, alive, fully present to the moment, I make myself available to be guided by nature rather than by my thinking. I assume that there is an ideal way that I do not yet know and that the more present I am, the more easily I will be able to discern it. By being present, I insist on guidance, and the universe will provide it for me. Always. And inevitably, I will learn something.

Today I will insist on being humble. I will insist on being teachable. I will insist on being present. I will insist on seeking the new in each moment.

85

Live Your Life Like a Prayer

David Hawkins, author, teacher, psychiatrist, suggests that the way toward a more enlightened experience is to "live your life like a prayer."

To live your life like a prayer does not mean to be pious. It doesn't mean to try to be perfect. It means to be in communication with life—part of the flow of love that is our birthright and our responsibility as humans.

The equation is this: We open ourselves to the love of the Divine, *and* we also open ourselves to the expression of that love in the world.

Every time we step into a potentially challenging situation, we ask for strength, support and guidance from this place within. And then we insist on offering as much love, compassion and non-judgmental awareness as we can to this other human in front of us. We wonder what we may *bring* to the interaction rather than what we can take. We ask for the grace to come from the heart rather than the intellect.

And when we are on our own, we ask to remember that the world is alive with the Divine in each moment and each molecule. We must keep in mind that there is only one thing, and this one thing is the very stuff of God—in the sidewalk beneath our feet and the way the breeze brushes the leaves above our heads; in the smell of the spring air and the quality of the light changing moment to moment throughout the day. We remind ourselves that this world that is God is as alive to us as we are to it.

To live your life like a prayer means to be in the conversation of life in each moment, rather than in the ever-repeating speculation of our self-centered, ego-driven mind. It means to choose again and again to connect within, and then to place our attention outside ourselves, and offer our attention and love to the world.

Today I will remember to live my life like a prayer. I will enter each situation knowing that God is within me and this other person; and God is in the air and the energy between us. I will ask for guidance from something other than my thinking that I might be of service, and I will be open to allowing love to express through me and to seeing the possibility of love in the other.

86

Playing for God

The flute of the Infinite is played without ceasing,
and its sound is love:
When love renounces all limits, it reaches truth.
How widely the fragrance spreads!
It has no end, nothing stands in its way.
The form of this melody is bright like a million suns:
incomparably sounds the vina, the vina of the notes of truth.

—Kabir, from *Songs of Kabir*
Translated by Rabindranath Tagore

One day I stopped at the Vedanta Center in Hollywood. Their bookstore is like walking into the past, in the best possible way, and I've spent many hours there browsing their shelves.

It was still 15 minutes til the bookstore opened. There were two or three others, like me, waiting outside in the sunshine. A monk (I assume he was a monk—he was wearing a very snappy orange sweater) came up to me and the young man seated next to me on the bench, and said, "There is someone inside (indicating the temple) who is going to play the cello. He wants to 'play for God.' He played for the Dalai Lama. I'm sure he wouldn't mind you listening."

I took off my boots and went into the temple.

Entering through the side door, I saw the musician—a big, healthy-looking red-headed man in his 40s, holding his cello and his bow. We exchanged smiles as I walked to the front pew of the sanctuary and sat. He closed his eyes as if in meditation, still cradling his instrument. I closed my eyes, too.

I had the thought that I'd like to see his first note and how he would move from silence to not-silence, but it felt more appropriate to keep my eyes closed, so I simply gave in to the deep calm of that space. I heard a few others come in and take seats quietly around me.

Some time later, I became aware of a sound, a tone that seemed not to have a beginning, but rather arose from the silence so subtly and incrementally as to carry the silence along with it; and as it grew in volume, it became recognizable as a cello note -- deep, long, resonant. But it was coming from a different place. I opened my eyes and now he was right in front of me. He had brought his chair to the front of the sanctuary and begun his playing in absolute silence, as if all of it were a part of his prayer. And now the music...

It was subtle and beautiful and profound, growing slowly into something, then subsiding, then growing again until finally, some time later, it disappeared back into the silence and we were left there together in the wake of it.

It was clear that there would not be another piece, and at a certain point everyone—the cellist and all those listening—stood. Whatever had taken place was over, and we filed out, bowing in thanks to the musician, smiling at him for the gift he had given.

How would we be if we thought God was always present? Where would we give of our time, our attention, our energy? If God were here, right now before me, would I still be worried about my bills/weight/career/social position? Would I ignore Him/Her/It long enough to check my email? Would I keep replaying in my mind the moment of shame/embarrassment that I've been torturing myself with for days or months or years?

The spiritual teacher David Hawkins says to live your life like a prayer, as if you are always in the presence of the divine. As if each moment mattered. As if the potential for beauty is here, always, just within our reach if only we choose to notice.

Today I will assume the Omnipresence of the Divine--here and now always, in each moment, in each space. I will assume that this Presence recognizes me. I will assume It loves me as It loves all that has arisen from it, with all the infinite power of Itself. I will assume It wishes to hear from me and has been waiting—patiently and smilingly—for me to arrive at this moment, exactly as I am, and give of myself to It by the beauty of my own presence. And when I forget, I will assume that the forgetting, too, is just a part of my song for the day.

87

Enthusiasm

Nothing great was ever achieved without enthusiasm.

—Ralph Waldo Emerson

The word "enthusiasm" comes from the Greek "enthous-iasmos" meaning, "possession by a god" or "having a god within."

Occasionally, life grants us an experience that fills us up, that pulls us out of the mundane and beyond ourselves, where enthusiasm carries us with no effort on our part. We do not need to wait for the universe to offer us this experience. We can seek it on our own, at any time. The translation from Greek tells us it's about God, but more specifically about finding God within.

When we are pulled into the stream of life and the joy of living, it's not the thing "out there" that we feel enlivening us, but rather it's something within that has been "turned on." The life force. The God force that insists we get present and offer ourselves to the moment.

The enthusiasm is ours to own. The experience of God within is ours to accept. I can stop looking for God out there, quit looking for anything out there to fix me or fill me up and look for God within. Simply by sitting for 20 minutes to begin my day, ground-ing myself in the inner experience. Then insisting that God fill me up. Possess me. Take me to the place of pure Being, of bliss itself.

Dear God, please use me today in the way I am meant to be used. Enthusiastically.

88

Unfulfilled Expectations

To carry an expectation is to have an appointment with disappointment. If we are disappointed in our life as it is today, it is because we expected it to be something other than what it is. If we are disappointed in our fellows, it is because we expected them to be something other than what they are. If we are disappointed in ourselves, it is because we expected to be something other than what we are.

When we allow ourselves to live in expectation, we can't see what actually *is*. We use expectations to give us an idea of future happiness: "I will be happy as soon as 'X' occurs." And when X doesn't occur, then I will have a reason for my unhappiness. I will have something to blame. My lack of happiness, though, has nothing to do with what did or did not happen with regard to X.

The Veda is very clear about this: Happiness exists only within. Nothing outside the Self can bring me more happiness than what I find within, nor can anything outside the Self take away from the happiness I find within. All happiness is self-referral happiness. If I have no relationship with my inner Self, I will not be capable of happiness.

My task is to know the happiness that I am, and then become present in the world. From this place of self-referral happiness, I can see the world clearly. I can see what is, rather than what is not, or what 'should be.' And I will begin to recognize the rightness of the world, of my fellows, of myself.

Everything, absolutely everything, is exactly as it is meant to be at this moment. To deny this is to choose to be unhappy.

Life is an adventure we are meant to enjoy. By being present to the unknown in each moment, we make ourselves available to this joy that is our birthright. We let ourselves and everyone else off the hook of what 'should' be happening. We let God off the hook for not giving us what we thought we wanted. We begin to have the life we are meant to have, full of happiness, meaning, service and gratitude; and when we have this, we realize it is what we were looking for all along.

Today I will let go of expectations and see my loved ones as they are, rather than as I think they should be; and I will love them for who they are, rather than in spite of who they are. And as I learn to do this with those closest to me, I will begin to find the way to accept and love myself, exactly as I am; and I will begin to accept and love the world exactly as it is; and the people in it exactly as they are.

89

Some Thoughts on Love

In discussions with meditators, three subjects attract the most interest: manifestation, love and death. Probably because the first two are associated with finding happiness, and the last is associated with losing it. So today, I'll take one of these and speak a little about it from the perspective of the Veda and the idea of life as a perfect flow of energy and information.

Some thoughts on love:

There is no situation that is immune to the power of love.

Any situation is upgraded by the addition of love.

Love is an action that flows outward, always. I can't necessarily feel your love for me (though I might find evidence of it), but I *can* feel myself loving you.

If love is needed in a situation, then I'm the one who must supply it. Remember, at the level of spirit, there is only one thing. I must be that one thing. Love is of the spirit, not of the ego/ animal nature. At the level of spirit, there is no other; hence, I cannot depend on others to supply love. It must come from me.

There is an intention living within me in every situation I step into. It might be to get you to like me or to win. Perhaps it's the intention to be so small no one notices me. Most of the time, these intentions are born from my ego nature. As such, they will never encompass every possibility available within a given set of circumstances, whereas the intention of nature or spirit will always be the highest good for all concerned. Whatever the intention is that's living within me, I can always choose to make it match nature's intention. That always will have to do with the capacity and willingness to love.

Love may not look the way I think it's supposed to look. I can love, even from the other side of the room, even if you don't know I'm doing it. Even if you've decided we're not speaking anymore.

To love, especially when we seem least capable of it, is to build a muscle that will serve us for the rest of our lives.

I do not need your permission to love you.

Today, if I feel hurt, challenged, angry, disappointed or lonely, I will take a moment, close my eyes, put my attention in my heart and envision a ball of glowing energy there—pure white light, alive and swirling—and I will send it across the room, the world or the universe to someone else, expecting nothing in return.

90

Eulogy for a Cat

Our dog, Butler, is still looking for the cat.
Or for the cat food.
She was a good cat.

Yep. She was. I miss her.

She had a good life. I have a great picture of her, out front, next to the orange of the lion's tail. Sitting on the flagstone path, in the sun.

She was sweet.

There are times when the Divine shines through everything...

I would say, rather, there are times when we notice.

Yes. Our cat died. Apparently, her name was Fire. Adele tells me she was called that because her mother was named Smoke. And as we know, where there's smoke...

I always just called her Cat.

She was a wild cat when I moved here. Feral, coming and going, disappearing for extended periods of time. Slowly, over the years, we became friendly. We left food out for her. She softened. Or maybe she got tired of fighting the world. She began to let me pet her. She began to make Butler, our Boston terrier, her friend. Rubbing up against him, pushing her way into his bed—never to displace him but to share the warmth with him. Butler, to his credit, generally took it without reacting.

More and more, she made her home on our back porch, lying in the sun, and coming inside and hanging out with me, until

Adele would notice and push her back outside again. She was a good cat. We were lucky to know her.

Now she's moved on. We know she hasn't just gone on a walkabout. We found her body under the house. This is how the Veda would say it. Not that we found her under the house, but her body. Because the being that was her is an expression of life. As such, it hasn't gone anywhere. It's no longer animating the body, just as each of us eventually will leave the body behind. But I will not die. Consciousness never dies. It merely changes form. Life doesn't end. It simply is expressed in a different way. We go on.

Even though I no longer have the great pleasure of petting Cat or hearing her purr, having her rub up against me as I feed her, the life in her that I loved has gone nowhere. It's still available to be loved by me. It can still serve as the target for that love. Just as I loved her before when she would disappear for days or weeks on end. I would think of her with love and wonder when she was coming back. This is just like that. I know I will see her, but it won't be in that body she had.

Love is the energy of life, shared between two individual expressions of life. Love is life in the one, recognizing itself as life in the other. And with that recognition, love flows. Naturally. Without choice.

The only choice we have is to ignore that life in the other; or tell ourselves not to love. We can tell ourselves that allowing love will lead to loss. The object of our love will die, move away or leave us, and take our love with them.

This is not possible. To be alive is to love, if we allow it. If we say yes. Nothing and no one, ever, can take that from us.

Look! Right now! If you have made it this far in this writing, then along with me, you, too, are loving the Cat, even though she has died. And doesn't it feel good to allow that?

Today I will let myself love without thought of return. I will love someone or something with or without their or its permission. I will look beyond all the reasons my mind can find not to love you and insist on seeing within you the life that is within me, and I will allow that recognition to begin the flow of love between us.

91

To Observe Yourself without Judgment

Our animal nature is a master of discernment. Survival depends on the ability to know what is food and what is poison, who is friend and who is enemy, what is safe and what is not. The proper use of this tool by our ancestors is why we are still here as a species. It's when we turn the lens on ourselves that discernment becomes judgment.

Our quality of life is determined far less by the facts of life than by the way our mind processes those facts. It's essential that we change the way we look at life. I can meditate from now until the stars fall from the sky, and I won't necessarily know how to choose happiness or even see it as a possibility. This is something that must be learned again and again. After so many years of negative thinking, it will take a while to train yourself to choose the positive.

The voice of the intellect we hear in our head often gives us a running commentary on why we feel the way we feel—processing the body's sensations and telling us what we should have done or could do to feel differently. It's constantly nattering about what's wrong with me or what's wrong with you. It's dictating how to get rid of our fear.

The mind makes this all up. And it always spins a story of negativity. When I listen to the story, I identify with it. When I identify with it, I fall into negative feelings. When I have negative feelings, my mind tells me a story about why. On and on and on.

It's a given that we will fall into this downward spiral of negative thinking. And it's our job, whenever we notice this happening, to interrupt the pattern, come back to the world rather than to our thoughts about the world and notice that some part of us is in fear, pain or sorrow. Be in the here and now with ourselves and recognize the sensation in some part of us that hurts and is uncomfortable. Just be present to it while knowing that what we truly are is so much bigger than this.

Today I will pay attention to the way my mind is working. When I find myself judging myself or others, I will pause, let the negative thinking go, and get present in the here and now. I will ask myself, who am I behind the judgment? And I will make a space of silence within to hear the answer.

92

Dancing Back and Forth

Two roads diverged in a yellow wood,
And sorry I could not travel both
And be one traveler, long I stood
And looked down one as far as I could
To where it bent in the undergrowth;

Then took the other, as just as fair,
And having perhaps the better claim,
Because it was grassy and wanted wear;
Though as for that the passing there
Had worn them really about the same,

And both that morning equally lay
In leaves no step had trodden black.
Oh, I kept the first for another day!
Yet knowing how way leads on to way,
I doubted if I should ever come back.

I shall be telling this with a sigh
Somewhere ages and ages hence:
Two roads diverged in a wood, and I-
I took the one less traveled by,
And that has made all the difference.

—Robert Frost

Upon their meeting, the poet Octavio Paz noted that Robert Frost lived away from people not to avoid life, but rather to see it more clearly; to know himself better and to hear his inner dialogue more as a flow of separate voices rather than a clamor of need.

From the perspective of the Veda, everything is a coming together. Each episode of life is an opportunity to love and recognize God in all things, people and situations. We learn to step forward into the moment rather than away from it.

From the perspective of our animal/human nature, everything and everyone must be treated as potentially dangerous and assessed for what I can get or what I might lose. Thus is born the need for judgment and separation, defining ourselves by who is against us as much as by who is for us, and withholding ourselves from the world and each other until we're sure it's safe.

Both of these perspectives are necessary for life to be lived through us, for evolution to carry us forward. To begin to discern one from the other is an essential aspect of our inner journey.

The experience of being a human is the dance back and forth between these two extremes. We step into life; we step back and regroup. We insist on reminding ourselves that "yes" is the ultimate answer. We insist on remembering that those opinions and ideas that tell us differently probably came from someone else—perhaps it's time to examine them a bit more closely.

Stepping back for a moment to do this is sometimes a part of the process.

Today, if I have thoughts of separation and judgment, I will ask myself if these thoughts fit into my philosophy of life; and if they don't, I will open myself to correcting them. I will challenge myself to step forward into the unknown rather than to seek the false safety of the known.

93

I Love You

Lamps burn in every house, O blind one! And you cannot see them.
One day your eyes shall suddenly be opened, and you shall see:
And the fetters of death will fall from you.
There is nothing to say or to hear, there is nothing to do:
it is he who is living, yet dead, who shall never die again.

—Kabir, from *Songs of Kabir*
Translated by Rabindranath Tagore

Around the world, it seems that cultures are splintering. The differences of one group compared to another are emphasized over the similarities. Perhaps it has always been this way. Tribalism, after all, is written into our DNA. But in the last few years, where there was once at least the appearance of a desire to coexist peacefully, groups are seeking instead to grasp as much power as needed to shut down the voices from "the other side."

In country after country, genocide and religious persecution are out in the open. The desire for equality by the disenfranchised is often met with rage and violence. Science has become politicized. News is no longer news but rather a question of who tells me what I want to hear. The idea of working together for the good of the whole has been overthrown by the need to separate "us" from "them" in whatever way necessary.

Difference and variety are the gifts of nature to itself. Rather than seeing our individualities as threats, evolution would have us see them as opportunities to grow. To see the world through your eyes for a moment is to offer me a more expanded view. And to keep my mind open to your concerns is how I practice being a better human.

It's essential that we honor the differences in each other and l work to make up for the inherent disparities within our systems—political, social, economic, emotional—lending support to those who struggle and recognizing the privilege enjoyed by those who don't. It's vitally important that we speak up where we see unfair treatment, where we see any group trying to bully its way into power at the expense of others.

But...

And...

It is only by recognizing that which underlies all the differences that we may ever hope to work together for the common good. We must make room for the variety of human experience but at the same time insist on seeing the place of oneness within.

The soul of me is the soul of you. You may disagree with everything I believe, you may live in a way I can't understand, but the inescapable truth is that you and I are the same. Behind and beyond all the contradictions, each of us is a pure expression of life itself. Consciousness is one thing. I am that one thing. You are that one thing. From this Truth it is impossible that I can hurt you without hurting myself, that you can hate me without hating yourself.

And... impossible that you can love me without loving yourself.

We are all in this together. To recognize and honor this in ourselves and each other is to begin to heal that which so desperately needs to be healed. I love you. Whether you care or not, whether you want me to or not, whether you love me or not. I love you.

Today I will look past my opinions and yours and insist on seeing that which is loveable in you, that which is Spirit in you.

94

Suffering and Gratitude

The wound is the place where the Light enters you.

—Rumi

Pain is a given. Suffering is optional.

—Anonymous

It's easy to fall into suffering. Especially nowadays, having lived through political upheaval, pandemic lockdown, unemployment, masks and social distancing. All on top of the usual versions of, *"Nobody understands me." "I work, and I work, and I never get ahead." "Where's mine?" "Oh, God! It's another one of those days!"*

The thoughts of suffering are habitual. We may be completely different people than we were five years ago (and if we've been meditating, it's pretty much a guarantee). Still, when we fall into our own particular malaise, the thoughts and feelings that arise today may be nearly indistinguishable from those we had back then.

As meditators, we must recognize these thoughts as evidence of stress release. Any thought that leads to the conclusion that I am a bust or that the world in some way is a bust is by definition a stress-release thought. It is the mind making sense of the negative energy and release of trauma that comes up and out of my system in meditation.

Nature does not think of itself this way. Lions do not berate themselves for eating the whole gazelle. Grass does not commit suicide.

When our thinking sends us toward the negation of life, we recognize it as the voice of stress release. These thoughts are not me. They in no way define who or what I am. What I am is a perfect expression of nature. By releasing these stresses within me, nature is clearing me of all that stands in the way of its full expression through me.

This may not change our feelings immediately. But by refusing to be defined by these thoughts, feelings and ideas of self, we at least allow an opening for the feelings to pass through us, as they certainly will do.

Then we get busy with life. We get present to the next task at hand. We take a look around at the people in our lives who have been at the mercy of our suffering selves—those who love us, count on us and need us to be the bright shining beacons of love and consciousness nature would have us be. For it is a guarantee that we cannot suffer in isolation (no matter how some of us may try).

And we become grateful to those who remain willing to put up with our shortcomings that arise from time to time and remind us that if we're still here on the planet, we have more work to do.

Gratitude may not be the opposite of suffering, but it is certainly a worthy alternative.

I am grateful for your hair, the beauty of your eyes, your way with words, your heart that always is ready to give, your willingness to grow, your willingness to not know, the way you garden, naked, early in the morning, your love of family, your love of wine, your love of pottery and tennis, your glass-half-full ways, your love for your son, your belief in God, your belief in the power of poetry, your belief in the power of love, your Catholic ways, love of your mother, love of Mother Divine, your pale white skin, your lips, your smile, the way you love your friends, the way you love.

95

A Showcase for Our Fulfillment

A relationship is not a place we go to get,
but rather a place we go to give.

The primary mistake we make in relationships is that we see them as a place to find happiness and fulfillment. But this can never be the case.

The Veda teaches us that a relationship is a showcase for the fulfillment that we *are*. If I am happy, any relationship I find myself in will showcase my happiness. If I am miserable, the relationship will showcase my misery.

If I believe that you, my partner, are supposed to make me happy, I will blame you for the unhappiness I feel. And if I am looking for you to make me happy, it is a guarantee that you are looking for me to make you happy as well. When this is the case, we're both looking to accomplish the impossible.

I cannot make another person happy. It will never be enough, exactly right, or last. It's a false construct. If I am living my life to make you happy, it means I have to pay attention to you to see how I'm doing. Of course, we are meant to connect with each other, even be influenced by each other; but we're never meant to be guided by each other. We are meant to be guided by our own experience of the truth as it feels and occurs to us deep within our being.

From that place of deep fulfillment and connection with my true Self, chances are I will approach you, my partner, with compassion and a desire to see you happy—probably with a desire to do nice things for you as a way to play in the realm of love. But the things I do will be based on my own fine level of feeling, instincts and the clarity with which I am in union with myself, rather than on how well I do in reading your mind.

As well, it's not possible to find fulfillment outside one's self. Never in the history of the world has anyone found lasting fulfillment outside themselves. Alexander the Great conquered the entire known world. Not fulfilled. Bernie Madoff stole *60 billion* dollars. It wasn't enough. There are actors who shall remain nameless, making millions of dollars a picture, yet by all observation are not happy.

Not power, not money, not fame. So maybe with love?

Many years ago, I saw a psychologist every week.. I remember once complaining about a lack of fulfillment in my relationship.

The good doctor said this: "Jeff, I have some of the biggest names in Hollywood come in here, who are married to the dream women of our era. Icons. Women in film and entertainment who represent to the world our modern version of the Goddess. And every one of these men, after six months with one of these goddess women, comes here saying the same things you're saying. What you're looking for doesn't exist. There is no 'happily ever after.'"

Our job is to know the fulfillment that lives deep inside the Self and then to find someone who is also doing the work to find that place for themselves. When we two find each other, there is an opportunity to build something greater than what the two of us as individuals could ever do alone.

With meditation, we find the fulfillment that we are. And when my fulfillment meets your fulfillment, that is a relationship worth staying around for.

Today I will remember that it is my job to learn how to love and allow myself to be loved. For this, the universe has provided me with potentially seven billion opportunities at every conceivable level of difficulty, from the easy as falling off a log kind of love we might have for our children to the are you kidding me type of challenge of the ex-partner, ex-spouse, ex-best friend who is telling lies about us. I will remember that there is no situation that enough love cannot heal.

96

Free, Present, Effortless Love

A *Course in Miracles* suggests it isn't our job to look for love, but rather to find all the barriers within ourselves we have built against love.

When we find it difficult to love, it is always because we are identified as the ego rather than as spirit. We have forgotten that we are spirit having a human experience and fallen into the misconception that we are humans having the occasional spiritual experience. From this identity, the thought of loving brings up the fear that we may lose something. Yet, what is there to lose?

The truth of the universe is its Oneness. The truth of me is my Oneness with. As the Oneness, there is nothing I can lose.

When I am identified as this one thing, love is free, present, effortless. It is my nature. Identified as this one thing, I am an outflowing of love. There is nothing I "need" from outside myself, for truly, there is nothing outside myself. Everything is mine to give. Love is mine to give. And because I am full, giving is all that I can do. I must pour myself out into the space around me, pour myself into myself.

Or... I am identified as individuality. As ego. Ego wants. Ego is empty. Ego needs. Ego is trying to avoid death, its own death. Ego will take and take, trying to fill an unfillable void. As ego, when you have something, there is less for me. And to give to you is unthinkable because I am empty. I have nothing to offer. And the little I do have, I must hoard.

How do we find our way from one to the other? By loving. By giving love. By going against all of the screaming voices in our heads and lives that say, *"Don't be a fool! Where's mine? Why does it always have to be me that gives? How dare they ask me for more! I'm tired of giving! It's time someone gave to me!"*

We hear these voices, thank them for sharing, and love anyway. In spite of ourselves. And by choosing to love, we deny the ego's lie of our emptiness, and we lay claim to the fullness that we are.

And we love.

Today I will make a point to give what I want to receive. Instead of looking for love, I will look for where I can give love.

97

The Power of a Broken Heart

a·him·sa
noun: ahimsa
(in the Hindu, Buddhist, and Jainist tradition) respect for all living
things and avoidance of violence toward others.

—Sanskrit, from *a* 'non-, without' + *hiMsā* 'violence'
Definitions from Oxford Languages

The thing most spiritual teachings don't mention about the practice of non-violence is the amount of grief you end up carrying when you let go of the anger.

Anger is not wrong, certainly not at this time in our world, for so many reasons. In fact, it has been appropriate, again and again, throughout these past few years. But anger arises and then subsides. It ebbs and flows.

It's only when we freeze it in place and assign it to one person, group or way of thinking or behaving that it can begin to eat us from the inside. When we start to believe that "if only so and so were gone," or, "if only such and such were different, then I wouldn't have this anger," this is an illusion. And the illusion is that we can actually gain control of others and/or the world.

If we are trying to find a spiritual approach to all of this worldly chaos, though, we will want to let the anger find its proper place in our experience of things, arising here and there, then settling back down again. However, when we do that, what comes up in us might be the grief, sorrow and broken-heartedness of seeing principles and ideals that we cherish torn down before our very eyes. We might feel the pain of every other disappointment we've had in life, the sadness we've carried with us from other losses.

Oscar Wilde said "Hearts are made to be broken." Perhaps. But spiritual truths tell us that everything happens for a reason, and the reason is always about progressive change. The evolution of spirit. It's our job to look for the good, to seek the next right step forward that can move us in the direction of that evolution. And to do that, we must find the willingness not to turn away from our grief or pretend it isn't there. We must never allow it to be covered up with the idea that it's the fault of the other and the anger this very idea may set off within us.

The depth of our grief is evidence of how deeply we have loved. And it's the love that the anguish uncovers for us that will show us the way forward.

Today I will let myself feel the grief I might be carrying, and I will see it as a call to love, rather than a reason to hate.

98

There is Nothing to Fear

What I am saying is that there is nothing to fear.
To live with this understanding is what is called holistic living.
It is to live with the understanding that the entire universe is
pervaded by that blissful Supreme Being and we are a part of that!
This is not a fantasy that needs to be worked out in our minds.
It is a fact and the actual process through which it is possible
is known as sadhana or meditation.

—Sri M

We are spirit, having a human experience. At any given moment, we are aligned with or identified as the one or the other—spirit or human.

If I am behaving from fear (or anger), this is evidence that my survival mechanism has been triggered, that I am feeling my well-being, or even my life, threatened in this moment. And now, depending on my individuality, I will go into a fight, flight, freeze or fawn response, lashing out or running away, becoming still as a mouse or trying desperately to please this perceived threat. It means at this moment, I am identified with the small self, the human self.

The firing of this system happens without my permission. It's triggered in the amygdala, which then informs my body that there is a threat. What I do with this message from the ancient part of my brain, though, is entirely up to me.

If my safety or that of those around me is being threatened, we can celebrate the fact that our system is working properly and allow it to guide us in our actions forward. If, however, the sense of threat is being triggered by the voice of a man who happens to sound like my father or by my perception that some authority figure disapproves of me, then the reaction is only going to interfere with my ability to see what could be the next right action for me in the moment.

To allow this reaction to define me, and take this apparent need to protect myself seriously, means that I am letting myself be identified as the animal nature of me, as the ego-self or small self. It's not wrong. It's just a mistake on my part as to who I actually am.

I have a choice. When this happens, I can let go of this ego identification, knowing that the sense of myself as spirit is here and available to me, whether I can feel it in the moment or not. I can let go of the fear-based identity and get present to the reality of a given moment, and choose to trust that the larger Self, the spirit of me and the universe, will be there for me to depend on. And that if I listen past the voice of fear, something within will guide me to the next right action, the direction that God would have me move in, show me that there is nothing to fear.

Today, I will notice when I am in a state of fear or anger, and I will choose to get out of my thoughts about what I fear or what is making me angry. And I will choose instead to be fully present in this moment and willing to give of myself to the world.

99

Everyone is Capable of Evolution

I am free of all prejudices. I hate everyone equally.

—W. C. Fields

There are days when other people in our lives feel more like problems than solutions. Maybe it's the next door neighbor who wants to cut down our tree because of the sap it drops. It could be the boss who 'has it in for us,' or the ex-spouse who won't be satisfied with anything less than blood. Or there are the people we get along with nearly always—except when they do that one thing, like the brother-in-law who insists on making jokes about bodily functions during lunch.

When trying to live a 'spiritual life,' we're supposed to love everybody, right? So what do we do about the ones who seem to go out of their way to make that impossible?

First, we don't pretend to love what is unlovable in them. We don't 'make a mood' of enlightenment to cover up our anger or judgment or irritation. But nor do we react. We keep from rolling our eyes or sighing with annoyance or conspicuously counting to 10 before responding. And if what they're doing is potentially harmful, we find our proper and safe distance from them.

Second, we don't put our attention on what's 'wrong' with them. Attention is a powerful force, and what we attend to will grow. So instead, we find one thing about them that is admirable, and place our attention there. We grow what is good. Maybe they took special care with their hair today. Maybe they're wearing nice shoes. Maybe they made the effort to say 'please.' It doesn't have to be much. (Timothy F. was a man I knew who consistently made trouble for me, but we were in the same social circle and so had to deal with each other. The one unique thing I noticed about him was that he always matched his socks with his shirts. These many years later, that is what I remember about him. Not our troubles.)

Third, we never discount anyone's capacity for evolution. Everyone is capable of change. Everyone. If someone is still alive, they can evolve. We don't get to write them off. We can't ignore them. We can't sit in active hatred of anyone. We want to find a way to treat anyone and everyone with dignity and respect, maybe especially those who make it difficult for us.

I will find a way to be of service today to someone who consistently makes this difficult for me. (This service may take any form, perhaps even the form of staying out of this person's path.)

100

Change is Inevitable

*Certain indeed is death for the born
and certain is birth for the dead;
therefore over the inevitable you
should not grieve.*

—*Bhagavad Gita*
Chapter II, verse 27

We are Spirit having a human experience. Consciousness embodying itself as these nervous systems, and in the process, forgetting where we have come from. When Source is forgotten, we are subject to the needs of our animal nature. But the spirit of us wants something from us as well.

Thus, there are two demands within each of us, always: the demand of the ego/animal nature for safety and comfort, and the demand of spirit/life for growth and evolution. These conflicting forces play out in us by way of the ego mind saying "no" to the unknown, and the spirit Self saying "yes" to the flow of evolution through us, the ever-unfolding now.

Spirit grows and expands

Ego wants to find the perfect picture of life—money, safety, love, family—and then freeze it. This is its nature. On the other hand, Spirit only wants our growth and development—continual expansion toward the fullest experience of life possible.

Life keeps happening, despite our best efforts to stop its flow. So if we are aligned with the ego nature, we will inevitably be run over by the juggernaut of life.

Nothing stays the same in the relative world, ever. My thoughts and feelings are completely different now than when I began writing this 15 minutes ago, and they will be different again by the time I reach the end. It is absurd to decide how I want them to be and then try to make them stay that way. This goes double for all those people in my life who I think should be some certain way. Never, ever, will they cooperate, except in moments here or there.

Our task is to become established in identity with the Self within—that place of no-change where we are at-one-with nature itself. This is the truth that, once found and embraced, gives us the ground to stand on and the feeling of stability to allow the flow of ever-changing life to wash over us without being at the effect of it.

This is the gift we receive in meditation: guided by our practice to that place of pure Being within, transcendent of the relative world, and then lifted back into life with an opportunity at each moment to choose which demand we will follow.

Today I will meditate twice and remind myself throughout the day to take my attention from the demanding voice of the ego so that I may hear the guidance of the quiet voice of nature that waits to be heard within.

101

Listen

The first duty of love is to listen.

—Paul Tillich

Sometimes it's difficult to listen to each other. So many thoughts to think, so much future to plan, so many fish to fry. We end up multi-tasking as a friend pours out her heart, giving our best version of an interested listener, but really just waiting for our cue to nod, say "uh-huh," or move the conversation along to something less messy. Then there are those times we just want to solve the problem or convince her she doesn't have a problem when indeed, all our friend really wants is a sympathetic ear.

Someone willing to pay attention to her and what she has to say with a loving intention.

Sometimes to do that requires effort.

But what better use of our effort could there be?

Love is a field to be entered. It's an experience of the deepest, most profound energies of existence. To love is to be healed. To love is to become more like the angels, more like God. To love is to be aligned with the flow of life.

When a friend, or anyone for that matter, offers us a chance to listen, it is a gift. They are offering us the opportunity to flow as the universe would have us flow. They are asking us to represent, for that moment, life itself.

Why on earth would we refuse?

Today I will be present to my world and the people around me. Whenever I have the opportunity to spend time with another person, for a minute or an hour, whether they are selling me a coffee or meeting me for lunch, I will set aside my concerns and worries, turn off my cell phone/iPad/PDA/computer and engage in the loving act of listening. And when my thoughts pull me back inside, I will choose, again and again, to be present. And to listen.

102

Truth

Truth will always be truth, regardless of lack
of understanding, disbelief or ignorance.

—W. Clement Stone

Truth, in spiritual terms, is that which never changes. Though it may be true that I am hungry at this moment, lunch will change that truth as soon as I'm satiated. However, Truth with a capital "T" will never change. That which was True 10,000 years ago is True today and will be True 10,000 years from now.

Science in the 19th-century was purely materialistic. The study of the truth of things was confined to what could be touched, weighed, seen and observed. With the advent of quantum physics, it was discovered that the act of observation itself affects what is being viewed on the quantum level. So "truth" now was seen to be made up of what can be seen and that which is doing the seeing. To understand "reality," we must understand the observer and the observed.

British astrophysicist Sir Arthur Eddington, one of the first scientists to appreciate and embrace Einstein's theory of relativity, was asked this question in a BBC interview, "What is the truth about ourselves?" His response:

"We may be inclined to various answers: We are a bit of a star gone wrong."

Stardust is the stuff of which our planet was made, pulled from our sun by the near-approach of some other star millions of years ago. And from this same stuff, we arose. Eddington then gave his second answer, as the question would have been understood via the materialistic science of the 19-century:

"We are complicated physical machinery—puppets that strut and talk and laugh and die as the hand of time turns the handle beneath."

And then, finally, Eddington said:

"But let us remember that there is one elementary inescapable answer: We are that which asks the question."

This is the science of the Upanishads and Vedanta. The study of that which asks the question. This is why we study Vedanta or any works that speak to the Truth of our being. This is why we read things in the morning or evening, before or after meditation —to suggest perhaps a different way of knowing ourselves.

We have spent years, even decades, seeing ourselves in terms of our job, bank account, love life, home, possessions, physical shape, intelligence, education, and so on. We don't need practice with this. What we need to practice is looking within. This is the process of asking *Who is the questioner?* And, *Can I find him/her now, in this moment?*

The more we ask this, the less we're at the mercy of the world. The relative world is all movement and change. Our thoughts and feelings, too, are ever-changing.

To define ourselves by any of this is chaos at best, insanity at worst. Instead, we might ask: *What am I that never changes? What am I that is Truth? What am I that asks the question?*

Today I will read something that speaks to me of Truth. I will ask myself: What is Truth for me? *I will ask one of my fellows what Truth is for them. I will ask of something bigger than myself—nature, God, wisdom of the ages—to point me in a direction that I could not think of on my own for an answer.*

103

Self-Realization

Sri Ramana Maharshi said that Self-realization can be found by giving up our habit of seeing the unreal as real, so that only the real remains. What is unreal? Almost everything we define as ourselves. He suggests two practices to move ourselves toward our Self-realization. One is to ask, "What am I?" The other is to love.

What am I? Am I these thoughts? No. Thoughts come and go continually, with or without my permission. Am I these feelings? No. The feelings in me will change by the time I reach the end of this sentence. Am I this body? No. This body is changing all the time. Not one cell of this body was here even seven and a half years ago. Every seven and a half years, the body completely replaces itself, cell by cell, including bones and teeth. Yet I remember being 5 years old. I remember being 26 years old. I remember being 40 years old. What is it that remembers? What is it that witnesses these thoughts, these feelings, the actions of this body? If I remain open to discovering what that is, I will be closer to finding what I am.

And then, love. Always. Not just when it's convenient. Not just when it's expected of me. Not just when it's with people who have earned my love. But always. With everyone, all the time. Whenever my head tells me not to, I have to set that aside and love anyway. Every time I fall into judgment of one over another, of me over you, of you over me. Love. Set aside judgment and love. It's not always easy. But it is always possible. Try it.

We meditate twice each day for about 20 minutes and get in touch with what we really are. Then we have another 16 to 18 waking hours in our day. To follow these two suggestions might be a good use of that time.

Today I will challenge my ideas of what I am, and I will insist on loving someone I find challenging to love.

104

Seva, or You Gotta Serve Somebody

I slept and dreamt that life was joy.
I awoke and saw that life was service.
I acted and behold, service was joy.

—Rabindranath Tagore

Seva is a Sanskrit word that means "selfless service," or "service to God." In India and here in the U.S., it's standard in most ashrams that members perform daily seva. This is working for the good of all, performing tasks that may not be enjoyable in the usual sense of the word. It's about setting aside personal preferences to become aligned with a teacher, with a set of principles, with God. It is a way of stepping outside of identification with the ego.

We can see it, too, in our churches and temples, in yoga studios: individuals performing work for which they are not being paid and that is not for their own personal benefit. In Alcoholics Anonymous, the concept of "selfless service" or "working with others" is the main principle underpinning the whole 12-step program.

In our tradition of Vedic Meditation, it is a time-honored practice to give service to one's teacher by helping set up or take down chairs and assisting at introductory talks. My road to becoming a meditation teacher began by simply pitching in when I saw something that could make things easier for my own teacher, leaving him free to counsel other students or teach them this meditation.

This practice of seva is so ubiquitous because it is one of the most direct ways to bypass our thoughts, opinions, feelings and personal desires, aligning ourselves directly with the flow of life that is always happening beneath the surface of what we think we are. Nature is always evolving itself. By giving selflessly without thought of return, we behave as nature does:

- Supporting another part of itself toward progressive change

- Loving another part of itself to help it love itself

- Uplifting another part of itself because it's the right thing to do

We can always find something or someone to serve. In fact, we are always serving something or someone, though perhaps most of the time it's something small and of the ego. This is not because we're bad, but because we're not focused on becoming aware of our motivations. Once we become aware, it's almost ridiculously easy to choose to serve selflessly. And the payoff is the joy of knowing ourselves as what we truly are: nature itself.

Existence, consciousness, bliss. Individual expressions of the one thing and aligned with the flow of the one thing, open to the joy of existence.

Today I will step outside the idea of trying to fulfill my individual needs, and I will give of myself to another without expecting anything in return. I will ask the universe what it would have of me, and I will keep my eyes open to see where I may be of service.

105

We Cannot Hate Our Way to Love, II

"Hate the sin and not the sinner" is a precept which, though
easy enough to understand, is rarely practiced, and that is why
the poison of hatred spreads in the world... Man and his deed are
two distinct things. It is quite proper to resist and attack a system,
but to resist and attack its author is tantamount to resisting and
attacking oneself. For we are all tarred with the same brush and
are children of one and the same Creator, and as such the divine
powers within us are infinite. To slight a single human being is
to slight those divine powers, and thus to harm not only that
being but with him the whole world.

—Mahatma Gandhi,
A Tussle with Power

Non-violence is not a garment to be put on and off at will. Its
seat is in the heart, and it must be an inseparable part of our being.

—Mahatma Gandhi, source unknown

We cannot hate our way to love. We cannot kill our way to safety. We cannot separate ourselves from an experience of wholeness. Life is one thing, and each of us is a part of it. And each of us owes it to life itself to support life always, in all ways, at all times.

Our people, country, and world, must begin to heal, regardless of the violence, cruelty, or perceived stupidity of those we would deem as "other." Though few of us might engage in physical violence, every thought we entertain of separation and hatred adds to the mix of the whole, lending permission to those who would seek to harm others. This is where we must begin.

If I cannot love my brother, I can at least remind myself that God loves him in spite of his politics. If I cannot speak well of my sister, I can at least keep myself from speaking ill of her. If the policies of those in power cause my heart to be heavy, then I must find a way for my voice to be heard in support of those policies that bring my heart peace.

Violence is not an answer that we may employ, ever. In this, we must stand together. The hatred must stop. It stops with me, now. And if it stops with me, it might become easier for it to stop with my neighbor as well.

Today when I find thoughts of hatred or animosity arising within me, for myself or others, I will ask for support from that power that is greater than I am to put my mind on what is right about my world rather than what is wrong.

106

Lifting Up the Curtain, I Have Seen

There is nothing but water at the holy bathing places;
and I know that they are useless, for I have bathed in them.
The images are all lifeless, they cannot speak;
I know, for I have cried aloud to them.
The Purana and the Koran are mere words;
lifting up the curtain, I have seen.
Kabîr gives utterance to the words of experience;
and he knows very well that all other things are untrue.

—Kabir, from *Songs of Kabir*
Translated by Rabindranath Tagore

Society, schools, churches, our parents—in so many ways and from so many directions, we are taught not to trust ourselves. We are taught not to believe what is within. We look to some authority or our peers to show us how to be, when all along, right here within, we are shown, step by step, where to go and what to do. We have the most perfect guidance system there could be if only we stop long enough to experience it.

We may ask, "What does your heart say?" Not: "What do you think? Or, "What is your opinion?" How would the most perfect world feel, and are you moving toward that? And if not, how is that working for you? Are you happy? Content? Are you choosing unhappiness now to have happiness in some distant future?

Inside each of us, there is a longing for something more than what can be seen and heard. There is the desire for wholeness, for unity. If there is something beyond chaos and chance in this universe, and if there is an intelligence to this life, why would that intelligence give us these longings other than to lead us in the direction it would have us move? Call it nature, God or flow, how could it be served by giving us unfulfillable desires, dooming us to lives of quiet desperation?

Nature shows itself the direction of life through desire and the feeling of rightness. Witness the blossoms of the sunflower following the sun across the sky or soon-to-be-lovers connecting across a crowded room. Notice geese flying north in formation with the spring or dolphins protecting surfers from sharks.

This is life asserting itself in undeniable ways. And if we look at our own lives, we can see there are times when we know just what to do, and by following this hunch or intuition, we find ourselves in exactly the right place at exactly the right time.

Even this can be discounted as a coincidence. But why would we? Play a bit. See the universe as here for your learning and your bliss, rather than to fulfill you or serve your ego needs; perfectly designed to evolve you as an expression of nature and guiding you within, always, to the next right action. This is the way the universe communicates with itself. It makes itself feel right when it is right.

Today I will follow an inspirational feeling, even at the risk of doing something silly. I will allow a sense of play and whimsy in my day for at least a moment.

107

Horses

O friend! hope for Him while you live, know while you live,
understand while you live: for in life deliverance abides.
If your bonds be not broken while living,
what hope of deliverance in death?

—Kabir, from *Songs of Kabir*
Translated by Rabindranath Tagore

My friend Lauren and I used to ride horses together. Twice a week or so, for about a year. I wasn't a big horse person, but Lauren needed a partner on her rides, and thinking my Montana pedigree implied horse sense, she nominated me as the guy to get her thorny horse in order.

Truth is, when I lived and worked in Montana, I was much more a farmer than a rancher (big difference in that world at that time), and whenever a cow or two needed chasing, I did so on a dirt bike, rather than on a horse. In those days, for me, horses were way too much trouble. They required attention, love, affection, humanness—qualities in which I was sorely lacking. But now, 40 years and a lifetime or two later, when Lauren asked me to ride, I didn't hesitate.

"You're a good horseman, right?"

"Oh, absolutely. Where and when? I'm there."

Why? Because I wanted to spend time with Lauren, and if that required me being a good horseman, then by God, that's what I was going to be.

When we rode together, time didn't matter. Problems didn't exist. She wasn't sick with cancer. I wasn't losing a friend. It was always springtime. The horses would stop and eat flowers, and we'd let them. Cheyenne, the problem horse, was not a problem for me. (I've picked up a thing or two, mostly from Jack Lilly and his sons, Hollywood wranglers I've had the honor to learn from on Westerns I've done.) So after a few test runs, Cheyenne let me be the boss.

Lauren and I almost never talked about anything deep or meaningful on our rides, but she was a meditator, too, and for those few hours a few times a week, we were together—me, Lauren, the horses, the sky, the day, the path, the moment—all one thing. One thing, and awake.

This is the power of consciousness. Some version of this is available to us all the time. This kind of sharing. This kind of one-ness. Why don't we always have it? Perhaps because it scares us. It scares us to think of having it, to let ourselves want it. (Because what if someone could take it away?) It scares us to think of letting someone else in. But guess what? They're already in.

In consciousness, this is the only truth. Oneness. We can make ourselves ignore it, which we so often do, but in truth, we humans are as intimate as intimate can be with each other, always. Sometimes we let ourselves feel it; and when I feel it, and you feel it, we call it love.

The last time Lauren and I went riding together, she called me at seven in the morning and said, "I'm just back from the hospital. I haven't slept all night. Haven't had a shower. But they gave me steroids, so I can breathe for the first time in days. Come. Let's go for a ride."

I was there in 15 minutes.

We rode way out into Griffith Park, let the horses drink their fill and graze in the shade, then headed home. On the trail back, there was a ravine. Coming to its edge, we paused for a moment. There's a path around the rim of the ravine, safe and serene, the path we'd always taken. And there's a path, steep, down one side, through the brush at the bottom, and up the other side. Lauren looked at me—God, I can see that look now. The beauty of it— and said, "Let's do it."

And suddenly, we were over the edge and down and riding faster than I'd ever been on a horse. The four of us were alive, together and flying. It lasted forever and was over too soon, and then we were moseying back across the L.A. River, past the stables and through the neighborhood to Lauren's, the horses seeming proud and fulfilled, and both of us with the silliest grins pasted to our faces.

Today I will allow myself to know someone as deeply as I would if it were the last time we'd see each other, and I will express my gratitude to the universe for the opportunity.

108

Relax and Enjoy

If we really understand what the universe is about,
we never need to fear letting go of anything.

—the author

We live in an infinite universe that is continually evolving. This is all that nature knows how to do: evolve.

We are nature. As individual expressions of nature, this is all we know how to do. Evolve. Even if it might seem to be something else, evolution is all that is happening, ever. Progressive change.

Evolution, for us humans, means becoming more and more what we truly are, which it turns out is expressions of the Divine, expressions of love. In an infinite universe, this will happen eventually, whether we want it to or not.

We're all headed to the same place: enlightenment. We are destined to be the pure and free expression of life and love that we are. This is inevitable. And in this infinite universe, the timing between when a saint or a sinner arrives at this place is less than the snap of a finger.

Today I will remember we're all headed home. The only question becomes: How much do we want to enjoy the ride?

About Jeff Kober

Jeff Kober is a teacher of Vedic Meditation, an actor and a wet-plate collodion photographer. He lives in Studio City, California with his wife, Adele, labradoodle, Bud Powell, and occasional cat, Pancho.

You may connect with Jeff through his website: www.jeff-kober.com

Acknowledgements

I offer my most profound thanks to these friends without whose help this book would not exist.

To Adele, for the initial inspiration for these writings and her unceasing support through the years.

To my friend and colleague Diana, for her wisdom, loyalty and her commitment to pulling it all together, and so much else.

To Trudi, for her eagle eye for detail, her generosity and her always uplifting spirit.

To Rainn, for his big heart, his beautiful soul and his willingness to share himself with the world.

To Anna David, every writer's friend, who told me to shut up and write.

To Melina, for sitting for the tintype, and agreeing to let me use the image on the cover. So beautiful in every way.

To Geoffrey Berliner and Penumbra Foundation, New York, for the author photo and keeping analog photography alive in a digital world.

To Heidi Le, for wrangling all the different threads of it together.

To Sri M, for his generosity, his teaching and his willingness to be in the world.

To Arran Russell, for his artistic eye.

To Trevor and Sylvie for their continuing soundtrack to life (and to the podcast).

To Heather and Onur, for making it all look good.

To Thom Knoles, for believing in me before I believed in myself, and for teaching me meditation.

To Ed Kaye-Martin, for teaching me the value of truth.

To TimBeau, for the right word at the right time.

To Chuck, for his willingness to share the music.

To Ashley, for her delight in the universe, the purity of her heart and her willingness to share it with the world, and with me.

To all the readers who have kept me on track with their input and support.

To Bird, for being my North Star.

Bibliography

Nisargadatta Maharaj. *I Am That: Talks with Sri Nisargadatta Maharaj.* Translated from the Marathi Tape-recordings by Maurice Frydman; Edited by Sudhakar S. Dikshit. 2d rev. ed. (Durham, NC: The Acorn Press, 2012, 4th printing 2020.)

Material excerpted from *The Truth Is* ©1995, 1998, 2000 Prashanti de Jager and Yudhishtara by Sri H. W. L. Poonja, used with permission from Red Wheel/Weiser, LLC Newburyport, MA www.redwheelweiser.com.

All Sri M quotes used with his permission.

Lightning Source UK Ltd.
Milton Keynes UK
UKHW011331210322
400383UK00004B/1156